The Kennedy Wit

LOUIS GRANT

EDITED BY BILL ADLER

The Kennedy Wit

A CITADEL PRESS BOOK
Published by Carol Publishing Group

First Carol Publishing Group Edition 1991

A Citadel Press Book
Published by Carol Publishing Group
Citadel Press is a registered trademark of
Carol Communications, Inc.

Editorial Offices   Sales & Distribution Offices
600 Madison Avenue   120 Enterprise Avenue
New York, NY 10022   Secaucus, NJ 07094

In Canada: Musson Book Company
A division of General Publishing Co. Limited
Don Mills, Ontario

Manufactured in the United States of America

10 9 8 7 6 5 4 3 2 1

Carol Publishing Group books are available at special discounts
for bulk purchases, for sales promotions, fund raising, or
educational purposes. Special editions can also be created to
specifications. For details contact: Special Sales Department,
Carol Publishing Group, 120 Enterprise Ave., Secaucus, NJ 07094

ISBN 0-8065-1234-2

Contents

Acknowledgments

I should like to express my sincere gratitude to my managing editor, David Curtis, and to my able research assistants, Catherine Johnston and Janice Van Raay, for their help in the preparation of this book.

BILL ADLER

Introduction

When *The Kennedy Wit* was first published in 1964, it became an immediate best-seller. It was quite apparent that
the American public, and people the world over, had taken
John F. Kennedy very much to their hearts. They wanted to
remember him not only as an able and determined political
leader, but also as a warm, charming, and immensely witty
man, whose sense of humor never deserted him even in his
most trying hours. In response to many requests to update
and complete my collection of the Kennedy wit, I have
gathered into this one volume all of the material in my two
earlier collections, and added to it a great deal more that has
come to light since their publication.

John F. Kennedy's wit was as much a part of him as his
hearty Irish temperament. It was the product of a quick,
agile, penetrating mind, coupled with an innate sense of
irony. John Kennedy had come near to death often enough
to understand at first hand the transitoriness of life and fortune. He could thus regard himself and the world around
him with objective detachment. He was never one for ab-

stract philosophizing—action was his strongest suit—but an insight into his thinking can be gained from these lines, which he had inscribed on a silver beer mug he gave his close friend Dave Powers for his birthday:

> *There are three things which are real:*
> *God, human folly and laughter.*
> *The first two are beyond our comprehension*
> *So we must do what we can with the third.*

As Tom Wicker points out in his *Kennedy Without Tears*, it subsequently took quite a bit of scholarly digging before someone found the source of this quotation, Aubrey Mennon's version of *The Ramayana*. But, significantly, John F. Kennedy knew it by heart.

The President certainly did a lot with laughter. He put his wit to good use during the long, uphill campaign for the nation's top post. Yet John Kennedy's humor was not at its best when prefabricated for political speechmaking. He loved humor for its own sake, for the way it breathed a clean, fresh spirit into all things. His most trenchant witticisms were spontaneous, featuring rattling, off-the-cuff repartee or clear-sighted shafts of ironic commentary. One example that comes to mind occurred during his 1961 meeting in Vienna with Premier Khrushchev of the Soviet Union. Discussing the delicate issue of the nuclear test ban, President Kennedy referred to an old Chinese proverb: "The journey of a thousand miles begins with one step." Noted Khrushchev, "You seem to know the Chinese very well." To which Kennedy responded prophetically, "We may both get to know them better."

John F. Kennedy's sense of humor reflected, I believe, a

conflict within him. His commitment to action, in the unfailing belief that circumstances could be improved, was often qualified by his understanding that human beings generally achieve only part of their goals, however noble. His ironic point of view started with himself. Although human greatness was one of his lifelong interests, his own political successes left him less impressed with his power than with the great responsibility he bore. Kennedy was often the target of his own most pointed barbs. Once, when a little boy asked him how he had become such a great war hero, the President replied, "It was absolutely involuntary. They sank my boat."

A tip-off to John Kennedy's ironic mental detachment was his practice of speaking of himself in the third person. At one campaign stop in 1960, he tried to elicit a kiss from the four-year-old daughter of his good friend Paul Fay. But the little girl would have nothing of it. She squirmed and wriggled in Kennedy's arms, while Fay pleaded and cajoled her to relent. Finally she placed a hurried peck on the candidate's cheek, and was immediately handed back to her father by an amused Kennedy, who commented: "I don't think she quite caught that strong quality of love of children so much a part of the candidate's make-up which has made him so dear to the hearts of all mothers."

So John F. Kennedy was well aware that, regardless of his power and prestige, he was still a man and thus subject to his species' faults, foibles, and failings. And he knew that the same was true of every man. This knowledge enabled him to deal with every person, from the humblest to the greatest, as a human being.

It also enabled him to have a lot of fun with anyone or

anything that was in need of some gentle but pointed kidding. Not even the church was safe from his irreverent teasing. At one dinner where he shared the dais with a prominent but rather portly clergyman, Kennedy, tongue in cheek, remarked that he found it an "inspiration . . . to be here with . . . one of those lean, ascetic clerics who show the effect of constant fast and prayer, and bring the message to us in the flesh."

John Kennedy's life was full of laughter, for he had been blessed with a wonderful sense of humor and a temperament that rejoiced in using it. He could laugh at himself and at his world not because he underestimated the value of either, but because he understood the limitations of both. The tributes and memorials in John F. Kennedy's name are many, but I think his own legacy of wit—with the lesson it holds for all of us—is a memorial that captures, more than most, the spirit of its noble author.

BILL ADLER

New York City

The Kennedy Wit

I

The Young John Kennedy

WHEN John F. Kennedy was thrust into the national spotlight during the 1960 Presidential campaign, it seemed to many that his bright wit had appeared out of nowhere. But the sense of humor Kennedy displayed as candidate and as President was no more unprecedented than his courage; both had been with him all through life, and had served him time and again as faithful friends.

The Kennedy wit had its recognizable traits even then. With characteristic irony and modesty, Kennedy enjoyed telling of the time when, as a youthful-looking junior senator, he was waiting in the Senate Office Building's elevator and "some people got into the elevator and asked me for the fourth floor."

The following are some more of the witticisms of a young man on his way toward success, already armed with all the requirements for greatness—including the gift of humor.

While an old friend of the Kennedys was visiting with the family, the dinner conversation unexpectedly turned to family finances. The subject touched a sensitive nerve in patriarch Joseph Kennedy, who became angered and immediately began a tirade against what he thought was frivolous spending by the younger members of the family. One daughter was his primary target, and before long she left the table in tears. She returned in a few moments, but the atmosphere was still tense—until John Kennedy settled the matter with this remark: "Well, kid, don't worry. We've come to the conclusion that the only solution is to have Dad work harder."

In 1937 Joseph P. Kennedy was appointed Ambassador to Great Britain, and the family moved to London. During the summer months of his vacation from Harvard, young John Kennedy came to visit and to travel around the continent, for a time joined by his Harvard roommate Torbert Macdonald. On one occasion the two boys rented an old broken-down jalopy to drive from Paris to the Riviera for a party. Jack drove as fast as he could, but suddenly he felt the steering wheel give a powerful jerk, as the car careened toward the side of the road. It hung on the edge for a moment, slid off onto the shoulder, flipped over onto its top, skidded for some thirty feet, and finally came to a rest upside-down, with its two occupants standing on their heads. With consummate nonchalance, Kennedy turned to Macdonald and observed, "Well, pal, we didn't make it, did we?"

John F. Kennedy's ironic wit stayed with him through all of his crises. As PT-157 finally located and approached the starving crew of Kennedy's wrecked PT-109, a voice cried out, "Hey, Jack!"

"Where the hell have you been?" he shot back.

"We've got some food for you," the voice told him.

"No thanks," said Kennedy, unperturbed. "I just had a coconut."

Joseph Kennedy is a legend in his own right. He is known as a competitive and curt businessman, although to those who know him well, he can be a very kind and warm man. He enjoys the exaggerated accounts of his toughness, and so did his son John. Both men often delighted in perpetuating the growing myth. When one of Jack's sisters was married, a newspaper reported that a member of Joseph Kennedy's staff had acknowledged, with a smile, that the cost of the wedding was in the six-figure range. The then Senator Kennedy replied, "Now I know that story is a phony—no one in my father's office smiles!"

During his 1952 Senate race against Henry Cabot Lodge, Jr., in Massachusetts, the "tea party" was one of John F. Kennedy's favorite and most effective campaign devices. At one such affair he told the women why he was so optimistic about winning the election. "In the first place, for some strange reason there are more women than men in Massachusetts, and they live longer. Secondly," he went on, "my grandfather, the late John F. Fitzgerald, ran for the United States Senate thirty-six years ago against my opponent's grandfather, Henry Cabot Lodge, and he lost by only 30,000 votes in an election where women were not allowed to vote. I hope that by impressing the female electorate I can more than take up the slack."

As senator from Massachusetts, John Kennedy received all sorts of letters from his constituents. One day he received a touching letter from an elderly lady of Irish descent, pleading that she was a shut-in and lonely. A television set, she said, would be the one thing that would make her life a happier one. Senator Kennedy was so moved that he wrote to his office in Boston, "Buy her a good used television set and send it over to her. She's a poor shut-in." A few weeks later Kennedy received a letter from the lady. "Never so insulted in my life," she ranted. "Imagine a *used* television set with a ten-inch screen from a man of your wealth." She had sent it right back and said that next time she wanted a *new* one with a twenty-one inch screen. And, she wrote, if it were not so far to Washington she would get right down there and give him a piece of her mind. Laughed Kennedy as he read her letter, "She's not shut-in. Somebody probably locked her in."

Prior to his wedding to Jacqueline Bouvier in 1953, John F. Kennedy attended a bachelor dinner given for him by his future father-in-law, Hugh Auchincloss, in Newport, Rhode Island. About eighteen of Senator Kennedy's friends were in attendance at the high-spirited affair. After seating himself at the dinner table, however, John Kennedy discovered that he was not at all familiar with the protocol governing the situation. So he turned to one friend who had gained experience at several such dinners, and was told, "the first thing you have to do is toast the bride—you've got to throw that glass in the fireplace."

The glasses that had been provided for the occasion were beautiful hand-cut crystal goblets. Kennedy promptly stood up, glass in hand, and proclaimed, "To my future bride, Jacqueline Bouvier." He drank the toast, and then announced gravely, "*Everybody* throw your glasses in the fireplace." In seconds all the delicate goblets lay smashed in the fireplace.

Auchincloss, in a mild state of shock, nevertheless ordered another set of the identical goblets. The new glasses provided and filled, the young Senator rose once again to his feet and pronounced, "I realize that this is not the custom, but the love I hold for Jacqueline Bouvier overcomes me. A second toast to Jacqueline Bouvier!" Once more the crystal vessels were drained, and again Kennedy declared, "And into the fireplace with the glasses!"

The next set of glasses were of the variety generally found in a 5 and 10 cent store.

Always youthful in appearance, John F. Kennedy used to enjoy telling his friends of the time when he was a young senator waiting in the Senate Office Building elevator, and "some people got into the elevator and asked me for the fourth floor."

John F. Kennedy's first known public speech was given while he was stationed with the Navy in Charleston, South Carolina, just prior to his tour of active duty. The topic of the speech was incendiary bombs, about which he knew little but had read much. The talk was a success, and emboldened by his warm reception, Kennedy asked at its conclusion, "Now are there any questions?" The first question was, "Well, you have told us about these two kinds of bombs; tell me, if one lands, how do you tell which is which?" Answered Kennedy promptly, "I'm glad you asked that question, because a specialist is going to be down here in two weeks, and this is the kind of thing he wants to talk about."

In October, 1943, Lieutenant John F. Kennedy was still recuperating from his ordeal after the sinking of his patrol boat, the PT-109. The story of his bravery is well known—not only did he save the life of a wounded crew member, but he also spent several days and nights swimming and wading around a cluster of islands in search of rescue. The following letter was written by Lieutenant Kennedy to a friend also stationed in the Pacific:

... Thanks for your good wishes on our rescue. We were extremely lucky throughout. After to-day it won't happen again. Working out of another base—I went in to see the Doc about some coral infections I got. He asked me how I got them—I said, "swimming." He then burst out with,

"Kennedy, you know swimming is forbidden in this area, stay out of the god-damned water!" So now it's an official order. . . .

Over and Out,

JACK

Commenting on his early days in the House of Representatives as a congressman, Mr. Kennedy remarked:

We were just worms over in the House—nobody paid much attention to us nationally. And I had come back from the service, not as a Democratic wheelhorse who came up through the ranks. I came in sort of sideways.

In 1952 John Kennedy ran for the Massachusetts senate seat against Republican Henry Cabot Lodge. He did not have the endorsement of a single important Massachusetts paper. However, the *Boston Post* suddenly switched from Lodge to Kennedy. Years later it was revealed that after its endorsement Joseph Kennedy had lent the paper $500,000. When the Senator was asked about it, he referred all questions to his father, who was able to explain the transaction to everybody's satisfaction. One reporter, having completed a discussion of the subject with the Senator, was exiting when Kennedy called, with a smile, "We didn't have a single major paper in Massachusetts. Hell, we *had* to buy that paper!"

As a senator, John Kennedy received a letter which suggested that Richard Nixon be included in the next edition of his best-selling *Profiles in Courage*, since Nixon had courageously voted against the labor unions on a labor bill. Kennedy replied, ". . . inasmuch as my book only included those who had passed away and Mr. Nixon is strong and well, the matter will have to wait for some years."

Remarked John F. Kennedy as a Senator, "I come from that section of the country where many school children have never seen a cow and the only things that farmers raise are their hats."

In 1953, as senator from Massachusetts, John F. Kennedy was a guest on the radio program "Meet the Press." A few weeks following the show he received a letter which congratulated him on his fine appearance but concluded, "It is unfortunate that supposedly intelligent reporters ask such ridiculous and impossible questions." The fact was that the "supposedly intelligent reporter" was a very close friend of Kennedy's and, unable to restrain himself, Kennedy passed the letter on to the reporter with the note, "I thought you might be interested in seeing the enclosed letter."

By the summer of 1956, Senator Kennedy's name was coming up more and more frequently as a possible Vice-Presidential candidate. Not too enthusiastic at first, Kennedy eventually began to take a more active interest in the possibility, due primarily to the constant urging and backing of his loyal supporters. When one of them mentioned to Kennedy that his support was coming from all over the nation, the Senator's reply was an unexpected one—until he completed his thoughts: "After all this I may actually be disappointed if I don't get the nomination. . . . Yes," he went on after a pause, "and that disappointment will be deep enough to last from the day they ballot on the Vice-Presidency until I leave for Europe two days later."

As a public figure, John Kennedy rarely showed his anger. Instead, he was usually able to give vent to his emotions through his wry wit. During one campaign for office he was stopped by a heckler who snarled, "Kennedy, I hear that your dad has only offered two dollars a vote. With all your dough can't you do better than that?" Kennedy replied quickly, "You know that statement is false." Then he added, "It's sad that the only thing you have to offer is your vote, and you're willing to sell that."

After his unsuccessful bid for the Vice-Presidential nomination in 1956, John Kennedy no longer held any ambitions for the nation's second-highest political post. Early in 1958, when a friend mentioned to him that he would have no trouble whatsoever gaining the Vice-Presidency in 1960, Kennedy smiled and said, "Let's not talk so much about vice. I'm against vice in any form."

During his political campaigns for the senate in Massachusetts, Mr. Kennedy was fond of telling the story of the little old Irish lady whose husband passed away:

She came to the ward leader with the complaint that the officials wouldn't accept the answer she gave to a question they asked her about her late husband, which was "What did he die of?" When the ward leader asked her what her answer was, the little old Irish lady answered, "Sure, and he died of a Tuesday. I remember it well."

President Kennedy's former personal secretary Evelyn Lincoln recalled one of the first times she met Kennedy—it was in 1952 and the then Senator was frantically getting ready to leave town for Easter recess. He was dictating dozens of last-minute instructions to his secretary. As Mrs. Lincoln passed he said, "Oh yes, one last thing. Easter Sunday." Mrs. Lincoln saw the girl's face fall, expecting to be asked to work on that day. "Yes. Easter Sunday," Kennedy repeated. Then, laughing, "You can take Easter Sunday off."

Having just assumed official duties as senator from Massachusetts in January, 1953, Kennedy wrote letters of thanks to those of his friends who had helped him during his campaign. To one he wrote:

Dear Dave:

Looking toward 1958, I thought you would perhaps like to have my ideas on your role in the next campaign.

What I would like to have you start doing, as of the first of March, is to collect as many workers as you can and ring all the doorbells in Amherst at least four times a week. Sometime late in October 1958, I wish you would drop me a line and let me know how you are doing.

With my best wishes,
JOHN F. KENNEDY

P.S. In your memorandum to me in October 1958, I would appreciate your including the names and addresses of all persons whose doorbells you have rung.

II

The Campaign for the Presidency

THE debate-like atmosphere of the 1960 Presidential campaign was tailor-made for a man like John F. Kennedy. He had the experience, the stamina, the intellect, and especially the tenacious competitive drive to match wits with a formidable opponent—and win. Once he had entered the race, John Kennedy's every resource was concentrated on victory with a spirit that had been instilled in him early and often by his father.

It was in this hard-fought race that Kennedy's sharp and ready wit became a potent weapon and an effective tool. Well-timed quips and good-natured jests often helped him deal with some of the most difficult issues. Not that he used his wit as a smokescreen, or attempted to belittle the issues with humor. But laughter did help him keep the pressure down, so that things could be argued reasonably.

Kennedy delighted in the stimulating give-and-take of the campaign trail, most often giving as good or better than he got. Once, when the Republican Nixon disparagingly called him "another Truman," the unfazed Kennedy replied, "I regard that as a high compliment, and I have no hesitation in returning the compliment. I consider him another Dewey."

The 1960 campaign truly offered John F. Kennedy the widest possible arena to exercise his formidable wit, and the quotations that follow demonstrate that he used that arena to great advantage.

When Senator John Kennedy was campaigning for the Presidency in 1960, his speeches were often sprinkled with quotes from well-known poets. One of his favorite poets was Robert Frost, and he would occasionally end his campaign speech with a few favorite lines from a Frost poem. While speaking before a group of students at New York University, Kennedy concluded: "But I have promises to keep . . . And miles to go before I sleep . . . And miles to go before I sleep." He paused and then said, "And now I go to Brooklyn."

In 1958, there were many Democratic aspirants for the 1960 Presidential nomination. Among them were John F. Kennedy, Lyndon Johnson, and Stuart Symington.

Mr. Kennedy liked to tell this tory about the scramble for the Democratic nomination:

Several nights ago, I dreamed that the good Lord touched me on the shoulder and said, "Don't worry, you'll be the Democratic Presidential nominee in 1960. What's more, you'll be elected." I told Stu Symington about my dream.

"Funny thing," said Stu, "I had exactly the same dream about myself."

We both told our dreams to Lyndon Johnson, and Johnson said, "That's funny. For the life of me, I can't remember tapping either of you two boys for the job."

I know something about Mr. Khrushchev, whom I met a year ago in the Senate Foreign Relations Committee, and I know something about the nature and history of his country, which I visited in 1939.

Mr. Khrushchev himself, it is said, told the story a few years ago about the Russian who began to run through the Kremlin, shouting, "Khrushchev is a fool. Khrushchev is a fool." He was sentenced, the Premier said, to twenty-three years in prison, "three for insulting the party secretary, and twenty for revealing a state secret."

Pikesville, Maryland
September 16, 1960

Mr. Nixon, in the last seven days has called me an economic ignoramus, a Pied Piper, and all the rest. I've just confined myself to calling him a Republican, but he says that is getting low.

New York City
November 5, 1960

Someone was kind enough, though I don't know whether he meant it kindly, to say the other night that in my campaign in California I sounded like a Truman with a Harvard accent.

New York City
September 14, 1960

During the campaign, there was only one occasion in which candidate Kennedy and candidate Nixon appeared at the same dinner. It occurred on October 19, 1960, at the Alfred Smith Memorial Dinner at the Waldorf-Astoria Hotel in New York City. These were Mr. Kennedy's opening remarks:

I am glad to be here at this notable dinner once again, and I am glad that Mr. Nixon is here, also. Now that Cardinal Spellman has demonstrated the proper spirit, I assume that shortly I will be invited to a Quaker dinner honoring Herbert Hoover.

Cardinal Spellman is the only man so widely respected in American politics that he could bring together, amicably, at the same banquet table, for the first time in this campaign, two political leaders who are increasingly apprehensive about the November election, who have long eyed each other suspiciously, and who have disagreed so strongly, both publicly and privately—Vice-President Nixon and Governor Rockefeller.

Mr. Nixon, like the rest of us, has had his troubles in this campaign. At one point even the *Wall Street Journal* was criticizing his tactics. That is like the *Osservatore Romano* criticizing the Pope.

One of the inspiring notes that was struck in the last debate was struck by Vice-President in his very moving warning to the candidates against the use of profanity by Presidents and ex-Presidents when they are on the stump. And I know after fourteen years in the Congress with the Vice-President, that he was very sincere in his views about the use of profanity. But I am told that a prominent Republican said to him yesterday in Jacksonville, Florida, "Mr. Vice-President, that was a damn fine speech." And the Vice-President said, "I appreciate the compliment but not the language." And the Republican went on, "Yes, sir, I liked it so much that I contributed a thousand dollars to your campaign." And Mr. Nixon replied, "The hell you say."

However, I would not want to give the impression that I am taking former President Truman's use of language lightly. I have sent him the following wire:

"Dear Mr. President: I have noted with interest your suggestion as to where those who vote for my opponent should go. While I understand and sympathize with your deep motivation, I think it is important that our side try to refrain from raising the religious issue."

In a speech before the Women's National Press Club, Arthur Larson, former director of the United States Information Agency under President Eisenhower, suggested that Senator

Kennedy switch his party allegiance and become a "new"
Republican. This was Mr. Kennedy's reply:

One temptation to accept Mr. Larson's invitation to become a "new" Republican is the fact that I would be the first
senator in either party to do so.

The public had a difficult time keeping the Kennedy
brothers separate and distinct in their minds, a source of
some concern and great amusement to John Kennedy during
the 1960 campaign. On one airplane hop from Boston to
Washington, candidate Kennedy was seated next to a lady
who turned to him and asked, "Aren't you afraid that those
terrible labor union racketeers will do something to your
seven lovely children?" Replied Kennedy, "That's not me,
That's my brother."

Later, as the plane was landing, the woman said, "I hope
your brother gets to be President."

"That's not my brother," responded John Kennedy once
again. "That's me."

Ladies and gentlemen, I was warned to be out here in
plenty of time to permit those who are going to the Green
Bay Packers game to leave. I don't mind running against
Mr. Nixon but I have the good sense not to run against the
Green Bay Packers.

Green Bay, Wisconsin
October, 1960

In Los Angeles during the 1960 campaign, Mr. Kennedy was facetiously asked, "Do you think a Protestant can be elected President in 1960?"

This was his reply:

If he's prepared to answer how he stands on the issue of separation of church and state, I see no reason why we should discriminate against him.

During the 1960 Presidential campaign, when the outlook was on the gloomy side, Kennedy would joke, "Do you realize the responsibility I carry? I'm the only person standing between Nixon and the White House!"

QUESTION. President Eisenhower has been a pretty popular President. How much of a factor do you expect him to be in this campaign?

MR. KENNEDY. Well, none of us are able to elect other people, unfortunately, in this country. But I do think he is a help to Mr. Nixon. I would be glad to have his cooperation, but I think he is already committed.

Hyannisport, Massachusetts
July 28, 1960

During a question and answer period following one of his 1960 campaign speeches, John Kennedy was asked whether he thought he would lose any votes because of his Catholic religion. He replied, "I feel as a Catholic that I'll get my reward in my life hereafter, although I may not get it here."

There is an old saying that a farmer votes Republican only if he can afford it. I don't think the farmer can afford to vote Republican in 1960. I think the farmer is in the position of the famous Mark Twain hero who rose rapidly from affluence to poverty.

Wichita, Kansas
October 22, 1960

How can any farmer vote Republican in 1960? I understand nearby there was a farmer who planted some corn. He said to his neighbor, "I hope I break even this year. I really need the money."

Grand View, Missouri
October 22, 1960

Raising funds during a political campaign is an essential part of our political system. During the Presidential cam-

paign, Mr. Kennedy spoke before many $100-a-plate dinners. On one such occasion, on September 23, 1960, in Salt Lake City, Utah, he referred to the cost of these affairs with this remark:

I am deeply touched—not as deeply touched as you have been by coming to this dinner, but nevertheless, it is a sentimental occasion.

One evening during the 1960 campaign John F. Kennedy was preparing for the first of several crucial appearances on television's "Meet the Press" program. Turning to a guest, he suggested, "You be Kennedy and I'll be Spivak." Immediately the first question sprang to his lips: "All right, Horatio Alger, just what makes you think you ought to be President?"

I understand that Tom Dewey has just joined Dick Nixon out on the Coast, to give him some last-minute strategy on how to win an election.

New York City
November 5, 1960

During the 1960 Presidential campaign, Mr. Kennedy suffered painful abrasions on his right hand. Continual handshaking had left it bruised, calloused, and swollen. He would quip, raising his hand and tensing his muscles, "With all that handshaking, this is probably the greatest right hand in America today!"

We had an interesting conversation at Los Angeles and we ended with a strong Democratic platform which we called "The Rights of Man." The Republican platform has also been presented. I do not know its title, but it has been referred to as "The Power of Positive Thinking."

New York City
September 14, 1960

I have been informed that with this dinner I am now responsible as the leader of the Democratic Party for a debt of over one million dollars. I don't know—they spend it like they were sure we were going to win.

* * *

There is a story about a Texan who went to New York and told a New Yorker that he could jump off the Empire State Building and live. The Easterner said, "Well, that would be an accident." He said, "Suppose I did it twice?" The Easterner said, "That would be an accident, too." "Suppose I did it three times?" And the Easterner said, "That would be a habit."

Texas twice, in 1952 and 1956, jumped off the Democratic band wagon. We are down here to see it is not going to be a habit.

El Paso, Texas
September 12, 1960

*Addressing a luncheon of Democratic women in Queens,
New York, on November 5, 1960, candidate Kennedy joked:*

I believe the Democratic Party can do the job best, and I
come to ask your help in doing it. There's an old saying,
"Never send a boy to do a man's job, send a lady."

Kennedy could never be described as a baby-kissing poli-
tican, and, in fact, avoided such encounters whenever possible. So it was an unusual event when, while campaigning
with his old friend Red Fay, he suddenly took Fay's four-
year-old daughter out of her father's arms. As he held her
she began squirming and eyeing him with long, suspicious
looks. Fay pleaded with his child to give Kennedy a big kiss.
Finally she gave him a quick peck on the cheek and strained
toward her father. The Senator immediately handed her
back with this comment: "I don't think she quite caught
that strong quality of love of children so much a part
of the candidate's make-up which has made him so dear to
the hearts of all mothers."

Last night we had a parade in Chicago for one million
people. I said to Mayor Daley, "They are all going to be so
tired from being in the parade that they won't be able to get
up on Tuesday [Election Day]."

*New York City
November 5, 1960*

The 1960 Presidential primaries were very hectic and candidate Kennedy was always on the go, so much so that he used to tell his friends:

Caroline's first words were plane, goodbye, and New Hampshire, and she recently learned to say Wisconsin and West Virginia. Any day now she is expected to come out with Maryland and Oregon.

Arriving in Wisconsin for his primary fight with Hubert Humphrey in 1960, Mr. Kennedy commented:

I am the first of an advancing army. By next spring the state will look like a college campus telephone booth.

During the heat of the 1960 Presidential campaign, Senator John Kennedy and a friend sought a few hours' respite on the golf course. On one short hole, Kennedy hit such a beautiful shot that it landed on the green and then began rolling straight toward the flag. His face registered pure terror until the ball barely missed the cup, rolling right by it. He turned to his partner in mock anger, "You're yelling for that damn ball to go in the hole and I'm watching a promising political career coming to an end. If that ball had gone into that hole, in less than an hour the word would be out to the nation that another golfer was trying to get in the White House." He paused—and added, "If that group of people hadn't been watching from the road, I wonder what it would have cost me to have our two trusted caddies keep quiet till after the convention?"

Ladies and gentlemen, this is the first time in fourteen years of politics that I have ever heard of a Democratic meeting and the Rotary Club joining together. I don't know whether it means the Democrats are broadminded or the Rotary Club is broadminded, but I am all for it.

Dayton, Ohio
October 17, 1960

I wonder when he [Mr. Nixon] put his finger under Mr. Khrushchev's nose whether he was saying, "I know you are ahead of us in rockets, Mr. Khrushchev, but we are ahead of you in color television." I would just as soon look at black and white television and be ahead of them in rockets.

Pittsburgh, Pennsylvania
October 10, 1960

I have been, in the last three days, in eight states, among them California, New Mexico, Arizona, Ohio, Illinois, Virginia, and the Bronx, the ninth state.

Concourse Plaza Hotel
Bronx, New York
November 5, 1960

Ladies and gentlemen: I said up the street that I am a former resident of the Bronx. Nobody believes that, but it is true. I went to school in the Bronx. Now, Riverdale is part of the Bronx, and I lived there for six years. No other candidate for the Presidency can make that statement.

Bronx, New York
November 5, 1960

I understand that Senator Goldwater sent a wire to Nelson Rockefeller a few days ago saying Arizona is in the bag. Well, it seems to me it is a mighty thin bag.

I was not aware that there had been an election here. Votes were not going to be counted until Tuesday, November 8th. Mr. Nixon has not got any votes yet, and neither do I. And I believe that if we keep working, we will just take Arizona right out of Barry Goldwater's bag.

In any case, we will make it easy for him to be a candidate in 1964. That is the least we can do for a favorite son.

Phoenix, Arizona
November 3, 1960

The success of a national political campaign depends a great deal on the efforts of the "advance" men. These are men who precede the candidate into a city to organize rallies and supporters. Although President Kennedy greatly admired the efforts of his advance men and their contribution to his victory, he always delighted in teasing them. He would point out that he campaigned heavily in Alaska and lost it, but never went to Hawaii and carried it. He would conclude: "Just think what my margin might have been if I had never left home!"

Dr. Topping, distinguished guests, ladies and gentlemen: I am delighted to be here again at this distinguished university. As a former student of political science at Southern California in the East, Harvard University, it is a pleasure to address this body.

University of Southern California
Los Angeles, California
November 1, 1960

I'm glad to be here because I feel a sense of kinship with the Pittsburgh Pirates. Like my candidacy, they were not given much chance in the spring.

Harrisburg, Pennsylvania
September, 1960

I recognize that the struggle here is not easy. I know that Barry Goldwater sent a wire to Nelson Rockefeller saying that it was in the bag for Arizona. It is in the bag for Arizona like it was in the bag for the New York Yankees.

Phoenix, Arizona
November 3, 1960

While we meet here tonight in the Golden Gate of California, the rescue squad has been completing its operation in the city of New York. Governor Rockefeller, Henry Cabot Lodge, Vice-President Nixon, and President Eisenhower all rode up together. I thought it was very unfair not to have Barry Goldwater along.

We have all seen those circus elephants, complete with tusks, ivory in their heads and thick skins, who move around the circus ring and grab the tail of the elephant ahead of them.

San Francisco, California
November 2, 1960

Commenting on the fact that Harold Stassen had announced that he would seek the governorship of Pennsylvania, Senator Kennedy remarked:

Mr. Stassen announces he will run for governor of Pennsylvania. He has already been governor of Minnesota. That leaves only forty-six states still in jeopardy.

For a short while, spirits in the 1960 Presidential campaign of Senator John Kennedy were dampened by false rumors that he had Addison's Disease. He did, in fact, have a very mild insufficiency of the adrenal glands, but it was nothing serious and he occasionally joked about it. However, one cold morning in a Chicago suburb as Kennedy was preparing to enter his car for a cavalcade, he spotted a certain reporter whom he recognized as one who had been particularly critical and suspicious of the candidate's health. Kennedy smiled at him and cracked: "You'll be happy today. We're going through Addison this afternoon."

During most of the 1960 campaign, a Republican "truth squad" followed Mr. Kennedy around the country, making speeches in places where the Democratic candidate had spoken. In San Diego, California, on November 2, 1960, Mr. Kennedy made reference to the "truth squad" when he quipped:

Now we have five days before this campaign is over. I cannot predict what is going to happen. The "truth squad" has been ditched. They told the truth once and they don't let them travel around anymore.

During the 1960 campaign there was some criticism in Catholic quarters of Mr. Kennedy's efforts to show that he was not influenced by the Vatican. Commenting once to the reporters about this situation, he joked:

Now I understand why Henry the Eighth set up his own church.

Any news photographer assigned to cover a political candidate knows that one prerequisite is the ability to muscle one's way through the crowds of other photographers to get to the candidate's side. In cavalcade, the photographers' car was the one directly in front of the candidate. It was always an endless battle between the "regulars," who zealously guarded their prized seats, and the "local" cameramen, who would frantically try to get aboard. At the end of the 1960 campaign several of the "regular" cameramen got together and built a replica of the photo car, using a tiny toy model. They crammed it full of toy figures, Scotch-taping them onto every exposed surface, and on the tiny back bumper they hung one perilously contorted figure. When Kennedy received the gift he immediately spotted the victim hanging from the rear bumper and asked, "Is that the local man?"

Mr. Nixon trots out the same old [farm] program. He has given it new names, Operation Consume and Operation Safeguard. But the words are the same, the melody is the same. Only the lighting and make-up are different.

La Crosse, Wisconsin
October 23, 1960

I shook hands coming over here tonight with some farmers—and how can you tell that they are farmers? It is because their hands are twice as big. I don't know what they do with them all day but they are twice as big because they work longer and harder than anybody, with the possible exception of candidates for the Presidency.

Grand View, Missouri
Otober 22, 1960

I don't see how the Flint High School football team ever loses any football games with that cheering section. If they are not busy for the next two months in school, we will be glad to take them with us all around the United States.

Flint, Michigan
September 5, 1960

Before the 1960 campaign, John F. Kennedy engaged Senator Hubert Humphrey in a very spirited campaign in the Wisconsin primary. Mr. Kennedy made reference to the primary when he returned to La Crosse, Wisconsin, on October 23, 1960.

I can make one boast that no other Presidential candidate in history can make. I have spent more time in the Third District than any candidate for the Presidency since George Washington. I chased Hubert Humphrey all over this district and never caught him.

Candidate John F. Kennedy's 1960 campaign reception in one city was deafening. The Senator appeared to have the entire population's support. Turning to a reporter in the deafening noise, he ironically wondered aloud, "Do you figure this was how it was for Dewey in . . . 1948?"

I want to express my appreciation to you for your generous reception at four-thirty in the morning at the airport. Back East, the Democrats go to bed about nine o'clock regardless of what happens, so I was very impressed, and my appreciation goes to all.

Pocatello, Idaho
September 6, 1960

On September 7, 1960, at a press conference in Portland, Oregon, during the campaign, Mr. Kennedy was asked his opinion of various labor unions. This was his reply:

I must say I hope I have normal courage as a politician and candidate for office, but I don't have quite enough courage to settle the dispute as to whether we should have craft unions or industrial unions. I will let you gentlemen settle that.

In a speech on the University of Illinois campus on October 24, 1960, Mr. Kennedy made reference to his famous television debates with Mr. Nixon in this remark:

A good deal of comparison, and most of it unfavorable, is drawn between the Lincoln-Douglas debates and my weekly brief appearance on "What's Our Line?" every Friday night.

I am the first candidate for the Presidency to actively campaign in the State of Alaska. There are three electoral votes in Alaska. I left Washington, D.C. this morning at eight o'clock. I have come, I figure, about three thousand miles per electoral vote. And if I travel eight hundred thousand miles in the next two months, we might win this election.

Palmer, Alaska
September 3, 1960

During one of John Kennedy's speeches in Cincinnati, the audience broke into laughter as Kennedy pronounced the city's name. He waited for the laughter to subside, then continued, ". . . and I am from Boston. *We* will explain to *you* how to pronounce it."

The 1960 Presidential campaign found John F. Kennedy delivering speeches from some very improbable locations. In one town he spoke from a street corner where the traffic seemed to be particularly chaotic. At one point, as a fire engine came screaming down the street toward his corner, Kennedy's voice rose as he announced, "Tell the fire department it is just Democrats on fire."

Governor Brown of California and I have been pushing a train all the way down from the Oregon border since yesterday morning and picking up olives, grapes, bananas, corn and one thing or another all the way down the rich State of California. I am reminded somewhat of an expedition which Thomas Jefferson and James Madison took in the 1790's, when they went on a botanical expedition up the Hudson River to find fish and flowers, and coming down the river they stopped in New York. They met Aaron Burr and the Knights of St. Tammany and they formed a link between the rural United States and the cities of the United States. They formed the Democratic Party.

Los Angeles, California
September 9, 1960

I remember reading when I was in school that at a rally in Madison Square Garden when President Roosevelt was running for a second term they unfolded a great sign that said, "We love him for the enemies he has made." Well, I have been making some good enemies lately. I find it a rather agreeable experience.

New York City
September 14, 1960

On a number of occasions during the campaign, Mr. Kennedy had trouble with public address systems. That is what happened in St. Paul, Minnesota, on October 2, 1960, when he joked:

I understand that Daniel Webster used to address a hundred thousand people without any trouble at all, and without a mike, so it should be easy for us. However, we are a little softer than they used to be.

QUESTION. Senator, you were promised military intelligence briefing from the President. Have you received that?

MR. KENNEDY. Yes. I talked on Thursday morning to General Wheeler from the Defense Department.

QUESTION. What was his first name?

MR. KENNEDY. He didn't brief me on that.

> *Press Conference*
> *Anchorage, Alaska*
> *September 4, 1960*

This week I had the opportunity to debate with Mr. Nixon. I feel that I should reveal that I had a great advantage in that debate and I am not referring to anyone's make-up man. The advantage that I had was that Mr. Nixon had just debated with Khrushchev and I had debated with Hubert Humphrey, and that gave me an edge.

> *Minneapolis, Minnesota*
> *October 1, 1960*

I know that there are some Americans and some Democrats who say that they have now developed a wonderful arrangement in Washington. The Congress is Democratic and the President is Republican and nothing happens and isn't it wonderful?

Alexandria, Virginia
August 24, 1960

Speaking in the Bronx, New York, toward the end of the 1960 campaign, Mr. Kennedy remarked:

A reporter asked President Eisenhower about a month ago what suggestions and ideas Nixon has had, and the President said, "Give me a week and I will let you know."

Will Rogers once said it is not the original investment in a Congressman that counts; it is the upkeep.

Alton, Illinois
October 3, 1960

We have the good fortune to have a member of the crew who was on my torpedo boat in World War II, who lives in this area of East St. Louis.

I would like you to meet my friend Mauer. He was on a merchant ship that got sunk in the Solomon Islands and then he had the bad fortune to come on my boat, which also got sunk.

Belleville, Illinois
October 3, 1960

What are we going to do with the Republicans? They can point to Benjamin Harrison, who according to legend saw a man forced by the depression to eat grass on the White House lawn and had only one suggestion for him—that he go around to the back where the grass was longer.

Springfield, Illinois
October 3, 1960

There is a terrible rumor to the effect that this is a Republican community. I am sure it is not true. But it would be interesting to know how many Republicans we have here today. Will you hold up your hands? Let us see how many Republicans with an open mind we have got. Two. Well, there is some prospect.

London, Ohio
October 17, 1960

During the 1960 campaign, Mr. Kennedy received two gifts from loyal supporters in Pennsylvania. At the presentation ceremony in New Castle, Pennsylvania, on October 15, 1960, he quipped:

I want to thank you for the plates. We will try to find a suitable house for them. We are looking now. And the golf clubs—I will be all ready to be President!

58

Senator Humphrey, Governor Freeman, gentlemen: I want to express great appreciation to Hubert. As I told him this morning, having to run against him in a couple of states is like playing Ohio State and then having to play Harvard. It is much easier to play Harvard after you have played Ohio State.

St. Paul, Minnesota
October 2, 1960

I want to thank that band. One more chorus of "Anchors Aweigh" and we will just float this building right out.

Akron, Ohio
September, 1960

One of the major Republican campaign issues was that Mr. Kennedy lacked the experience necessary for the Presidency. Mr. Kennedy had this to say about that issue in a political speech in Minneapolis in October, 1960:

Ladies and gentlemen, the outstanding news story of this week was not the events of the United Nations or even the Presidential campaign. It was a story coming out of my own city of Boston that Ted Williams of the Boston Red Sox had retired from baseball. It seems that at forty-two he was too old. It shows that perhaps experience isn't enough.

In the U.S. Senate, we are given the responsibility of ratifying treaties and confirming Presidential appointments. The

House of Representatives, however, is given far greater power. They are given the power to levy taxes and appropriate money.

So any time you don't like the way your money is being spent or what the taxes are, do not write to Senator Humphrey or me, but write to Congressman Karth.

St. Paul, Minnesota
October 2, 1960

Senator Humphrey, Mrs. Roosevelt, Senator Lehman, Mayor Wagner, Governor Harriman, Senator Morse, Congressman Celler, Governor Williams, Senator Hart—whom have we omitted? So many chiefs are assembled with so few Indians, up here and in the audience.

You can tell who isn't running for office by that relaxed posture they assume up here. Hubert and I are the only ones on edge.

New York City
October 12, 1960

I am here to pay tribute to a great South Carolinian—the New York Yankees' Bobby Richardson. Apparently he is one Yankee who has your blessings, and I am here to gain them too.

Columbia, South Carolina
October 10, 1960

While addressing a crowd of students at New York University during the 1960 Presidential campaign, Senator Kennedy was continuously heckled by a crowd of youthful Nixon supporters. They began to interrupt him with chants of "We want Nixon." Kennedy replied "I don't think you're going to get him, though." He then concluded his speech by addressing several remarks to "all you young Nixonites—all eight of you."

While on the campaign trail, Mr. Kennedy always attracted great numbers of very young people to hear his speeches. In Girard, Ohio, on October 9, 1960, the audience was particularly young, and he quipped:

If we can lower the voting age to nine, we are going to sweep the state.

I want to give you the best two-horse parlay in the State of Kentucky today. That is Western Kentucky State College in the winter and the Democratic Party in November.

Bowling Green, Kentucky
October 8, 1960

During the final days of the 1960 Presidential campaign, pro-Nixon hecklers were the target of Democrat John Kennedy's wit. To one Nixon picket, sitting on a telephone pole, Kennedy called out, "if you just stay up there until November 9 we can settle this whole matter."

Much was said during the campaign about the relative experience of Mr. Kennedy and Mr. Nixon. On this point, Mr. Kennedy made these remarks in a speech in Jacksonville, Florida, in October, 1960:

I know a banker who served thirty years as president of a bank. He had more experience, until his bank went broke, than any other banker in Massachusetts. But if I ever go into the banking business, I do not plan to hire him, and he knows the operation from top to bottom.

John Kennedy was a tough adversary in the Presidential campaign. He briefed himself daily on Republican candidate Nixon's latest speeches and attacked them continually. On one occasion, while before a large crowd of Trumanites, Kennedy declared: "Last Thursday night Mr. Nixon dismissed me as 'another Truman.' I regard that as a high compliment, and I have no hesitation in returning the compliment. I consider him another Dewey."

It is, I think, a source of concern to us all that the first dogs carried around in outer space were not named Rover and Fido but instead were named Belka and Strelka. It was not named Checkers,* either.

Muskegon, Michigan
September 5, 1960

* The Nixon family dog.

Addressing a "Breakfast with Kennedy" rally in Erie, Pennsylvania, on September 28, 1960, Mr. Kennedy remarked:

It always warms the hearts of the Democrats to see contributors gathered in one room on an occasion such as this. I wish there were some other way to run a campaign, but this is what makes the mare go and this is what keeps us moving today from here to Buffalo and on through New York. You would not have wanted to have gotten a telegram from Albany saying we were stranded there.

Former President Harry S Truman was not a staunch Kennedy supporter prior to the 1960 Democratic Convention. However, after Kennedy received the nomination, Mr. Truman threw his enthusiastic support behind the senator from Massachusetts. During the campaign, Senator Kennedy visited Mr. Truman at his home in Independence, Missouri. On August 21, 1960, he was asked at a press conference in Des Moines, Iowa, shortly after his visit, "How do the Kennedy-Truman ranks stand after your Missouri trip?"

They are as one, I am glad to say. I hope that I can do as well as he did. He told me all about how he did it. I hope I will come out as well as he did.

This isn't the way they told me it was when I first decided to run for the Presidency. After reading about the schedules of the President, I thought we all stayed in bed until ten or eleven and then got out and drove around.

Rockford, Illinois
October 24, 1960

Prior to the nomination of Lyndon Johnson as the Democratic Vice-Presidential candidate, there were rumors that Governor Pat Brown of California was interested in the nomination. This presented problems for Mr. Kennedy, because Governor Brown is also a Catholic. And, needless to say, two Catholics running on the same ticket certainly is not a balanced ticket. In a speech in California, prior to the Convention, Mr. Kennedy had this to say about Governor Brown:

I know there has been talk out here about a Kennedy-Brown ticket, and I sincerely wish that we could arrange that. Unfortunately, I come from Massachusetts and the Governor comes from California, and I don't believe the country is ready for a ticket that stretches from the Atlantic to the Pacific.

I appreciate your welcome. As the cow said to the Maine farmer, "Thank you for a warm hand on a cold morning."

Los Angeles, California
November 2, 1960

At a political rally in Rochester, New York, on September 28, 1960, the Democratic Party standard bearer quipped:

I am informed by someone with a long memory that when another Presidential candidate, Mr. Thomas Dewey, came here in 1948, he said, "It is good to be back in Syracuse."

He didn't know where he was going or where he was—and I don't think the Republicans do today.

The Republicans have run this century: Mr. McKinley, Harding—do you know what his slogan was?—"Return to Normalcy", "Keep cool with Coolidge"; "A Chicken in Every Pot" with Herbert Hoover. I don't know what Dewey's slogan was because we never really found out.

Wilkes-Barre, Pennsylvania
October, 1960

I was informed when I started out this morning that we were going to travel in Delaware County, which voted 8 to 1 for Alf Landon. We are going to wipe that record out. No county in the United States should have that reputation.

Norristown, Pennsylvania
October 29, 1960

John Kennedy's Presidential campaign was a hectic one, leaving the Senator little time for leisure. He would speak from breakfast to midnight, traveling from one city or state to another. He told one audience that each day "I look down at the schedule and there's five minutes alloted for the candidate to eat and rest." Another time, he urged the providing of medical care for the aged "especially as we are all aging very fast these days." And on November 3, 1960, as the campaign drew to a close, he said, "I am going to last about five more days. But that is time enough."

Speaking at a political rally in Lockport, New York, on September 28, 1960, Mr. Kennedy was aware of the fact that the city's mayor was a staunch Republican. The mayor was in the audience when Mr. Kennedy made these remarks.

I understand, Mr. Mayor, that you are a member of another active party in the United States. I hope you won't feel I am abusing the hospitality of the city if I say a few good words on behalf of the Democratic Party.

First, we will not rely on a monetary policy that puts its emphasis on tight money and tight interest rates. The fact of the matter is, as Frank Church said in his keynote speech, if Rip Van Winkle went to sleep and he woke up and he wanted to know whether the Republicans or the Democrats were in office, he would just say "How high are the interest rates?"

Saginaw, Michigan
October 14, 1960

I do not want it said of our generation what T. S. Eliot wrote in his poem, "The Rock"—"and the wind shall say: 'these were decent people, their only monument the asphalt road and a thousand lost golf balls.'" We can do better than that.

Columbus, Ohio
October 17, 1960

During the 1960 Presidential campaign, Senator Kennedy had substantial reason to worry about his popularity in several major states. In a letter to one friend he wrote, "As for Wisconsin, I am reminded of the story of the old Frenchman who was asked what he had done during the French Revolution. He replied, 'I survived.' That's the way I feel about Wisconsin."

To another he wrote: "Thank you for the cognac. I would like to say that I am planning to keep it to sip during the warm spring nights. Unfortunately last night I began to think about West Virginia and drank the whole bottle."

During the 1960 Presidential campaign a reporter telephoned Kennedy to ask, "Do you plan on taking your rocking chair with you to the White House if you are elected President?" Replied Kennedy, "Whither I goest—it goes."

During the 1960 campaign, candidate Kennedy always seemed to be hours behind schedule. He made reference to this on September 23, 1960, in a Wyoming speech when he remarked:

I first of all want to express on behalf of my sister and myself our great gratitude to all of you for being kind enough to have this breakfast and make it almost lunch.

I think the State of Iowa has an opportunity to continue the same kind of responsible government which Governor Loveless has given this state, when you elect Nick McManus the next governor of the State of Iowa. I hope you will send a young man down there to represent this district. This ticket is well balanced—O'Brien, McManus and Kennedy.

I hope you elect Congressman O'Brien, and I don't hold his name against him.

Sioux City, Iowa
September 21, 1960

I want to express my great appreciation to all of you for your kindness in coming out and giving us a warm Hoosier welcome. I understand that this town suffered a misfortune this morning, when the bank was robbed. I am confident that the *Indianapolis Star* will say "Democrats Arrive and Bank Robbed."

Anderson, Indiana
October 5, 1960

I come to Suffolk County and ask your help. If we can do
well in this county, and I ask your help in doing well, we're
going to put this speech to music and make a fortune out of
it.

Commack, Long Island, New York
November 6, 1960

During the 1960 Presidential campaign, John Kennedy
rounded up as many of his war-time friends as possible—he
wanted his war record well covered. At one gathering, before a large audience, several of these friends had introduced
one another with a brief description of their role in the candidate's war experiences. The final friend, nicknamed "Dirty
John" was introduced thus: "John wasn't in PT's but he was
there in his airplane—flying around looking out for us." A
moment later the candidate—waiting for the applause to
abate after his own introduction—stepped back from the
microphone and whispered to the group: "At any future
gathering of this collection of war heroes, let's make sure we
take Dirty John out of the sky and put him on one of the
boats. We can't afford to take the risk of possibly belittling
the great war record of the candidate by bringing in another
dimension."

*One of the problems of a political campaign is that the
candidate must be prepared to make a political speech at*

any time of day. John Kennedy referred to this problem in a
speech in Anchorage, Alaska, in September, 1960.

I want to express my appreciation for that warm Alaskan welcome. As Bob Bartlett said, we started out about nine o'clock in the morning from Baltimore and it is now four o'clock in the morning for those of us living on Eastern time. I have not made a speech that late in the evening since some of the early Massachusetts political banquets which I attended when I was first a congressman, when they would put the junior members on about this hour.

Ladies and gentlemen, this is the third year in a row that I have been honored by being invited to this steer roast, and I hope that it is going to be possible for me to come back next year in a somewhat different capacity.

Cleveland, Ohio
September 25, 1960

QUESTION. Are you going to change West Virginia's diet from beans to strawberries?

MR. KENNEDY. I am told you raise the finest strawberries in the world, so I am for it. We will send a few cranberries down from Massachusetts.

Charleston, West Virginia
September 19, 1960

Back in 1949 John Kennedy had made some critical remarks concerning the American Legion. So during the 1960 Presidential campaign, Republicans at the American Legion Convention which Kennedy was to address enthusiastically circulated copies of his attack. During his introductory remarks Kennedy wryly quipped: "I have learned a great deal about the Legion—especially since 1949."

At a press conference in Charleston, West Virginia, on September 19, 1960, Mr. Kennedy was asked if he would speak slower, to which he replied:

You are talking to a Yankee now. I suppose that is what my accent sounds like down here.

QUESTION. I am for Mr. Kennedy. And may I visit you when you are the President of the United States in the White House? I have tried three times and cannot get in.

MR. KENNEDY. Let's meet outside and we will get it all set.

Charleston, West Virginia
September 19, 1960

Ten years ago, as a Congressman, I came to this city at one o'clock in the morning for a Democratic rally and you were all here then. I don't know whether you have left this hall in the last ten years, but only in this city could they get a turn-out for a Democratic candidate at eight in the morning or at midnight. That is the kind of Democratic city to have.

Jersey City, New Jersey
September 15, 1960

During the campaign, Kennedy often remarked about the long and tough role of campaigning. He made these remarks on that subject in a speech in Dayton, Ohio, October 17, 1960:

Franklin Roosevelt started his campaign here in Ohio. I don't know what has happened to politics, but whenever I read about the 1932 campaign, Franklin Roosevelt stayed in Albany all winter, spring, summer, didn't go to the convention until he was nominated. He then took a boating trip up the coast of Maine with his son, started his campaign late in September, made some speeches, and was elected by a tremendous majority.

I personally have lived through ten Presidential campaigns, but I must say the eleventh makes me feel like I lived through twenty-five.

New York City
September 14, 1960

Ladies and gentlemen, the devices which are used in the City of New York to separate you from your life savings are numerous. When the dinners run out, the luncheons begin, and when the luncheons run out, the breakfasts begin. We may all meet next week to get the campaign out of the red with a midnight brunch at eighty-five dollars per person—and I will be there.

New York City
November 5, 1960

This port, this city, has been a great launching site for ships, missiles, and planes, and you're about to launch me into orbit over Texas, later this afternoon.

San Diego, California
September 11, 1960

Speaking to the Protestant Ministerial Association of Greater Houston on September 12, 1960, candidate Kennedy remarked:

I want you to know that I am grateful to you for inviting me tonight. I am sure I have made no converts to my church.

I want to express my appreciation to the Governor. Every time he introduces me as the potentially greatest President in the history of the United States, I always think perhaps he is overstating it one or two degrees. George Washington wasn't a bad President and I do want to say a word for Thomas Jefferson. But, otherwise, I will accept the compliment.

Muskegon, Michigan
September 5, 1960

Ladies and gentlemen, it is my understanding that the last candidate for the Presidency to visit this community in a Presidential year was Herbert Hoover in 1928.

President Hoover initiated on the occasion of his visit the slogan "Two chickens for every pot," and it is no accident that no Presidential candidate has ever dared to come back to this community since.

Bristol, Tennessee
September 21, 1960

I am very grateful to be the guest of Eastern Carolina College. I understand that they have had a most rapid growth and now wish to play in the Southern Conference. I am scheduled to play in the Southern Conference, too, and find it somewhat difficult. I hope you have success and that I do well also.

Greenville, North Carolina
September 17, 1960

QUESTION. Senator, Governor Pat Brown today issued a very optimistic statement. Yet a poll shows Nixon running ahead. Which of these two experts do you believe?

MR. KENNEDY. I believe Governor Brown.

Burbank, California
September 9, 1960

I come from a non-agricultural state, Massachusetts, and therefore, I am sure that there are some farmers in Iowa and South Dakota who say, "Why should we elect someone from New England? Why shouldn't we elect a farmer?" Well, there is no farmer up for the office this year. Whittier, California, is not one of the great agricultural sections of the United States.

Sioux City, Iowa
September 21, 1960

I want to express my appreciation to all of you for having come down to the station to meet us. Today we celebrate the one hundred and tenth anniversary of the admission of the State of California into the Union. It seems to me that the great story of California has come about because people were not satisfied with things as they were. They liked Massachsuetts and they liked Ohio and they liked Oklahoma, but they thought they could do better when they came to California. I don't know why they felt that way about Massachusetts.

Modesto, California
September 9, 1960

The 1960 Presidential campaign fostered many rumors that certain Catholic clerics, as well as many non-Catholics were opposed to John Kennedy's candidacy. Since there was never any real evidence of such Catholic opposition, the candidate's only reference to the controversy was this quip:

"They're working on a package deal—if the Electoral College can be changed into an interdenominational school, they'll open up the College of Cardinals."

Ladies and gentlemen, I want to express my appreciation to all of you for being kind enough to wait at the airport for my sister and myself, and also my regrets for being so late. In case any of you wanted to run for the Presidency, I would say we started this morning in Iowa, we spoke in South Dakota, we speak now in North Dakota, we speak at a dinner meeting in Montana, and end up in Wyoming tonight. I think that my election chief thinks that the election is October 8 rather than November 8.

Fargo, North Dakota
September 22, 1960

Last week a noted clergyman was quoted as saying that our society may survive in the event of my election but it certainly won't be what it was. I would like to think he was complimenting me, but I'm not sure he was.

New York City
September 14, 1960

Candidate Kennedy's wife was not able to accompany him on the campaign trail because she was expecting a child. On September 7, 1960, in Salem, Oregon, Mr. Kennedy alluded to this fact when he said:

Ladies and gentlemen, first of all I would like to introduce my sister, who is representing my wife, who is otherwise committed.

Ladies and gentlemen, I have been informed that the object in front of me is a model of a small potato grown in this county last year. I have been under the impression that it was a new Snark missile which was about to go in the state, but I am going to take everybody's word for it.

Presque Isle, Maine
September 2, 1960

QUESTION. Senator, do you feel that strong personalities, such as President Eisenhower and Governor Rockefeller, campaigning against you will be perhaps a severe handicap in your campaign?

MR. KENNEDY. No.

QUESTION. Why?

MR. KENNEDY. I think that President Eisenhower is not running this year, and Governor Rockefeller was not nominated.

I agree that President Eisenhower would be a strong candidate if he was running.

QUESTION. Do you feel that some of this might rub off?

MR. KENNEDY. I don't know. We will know in November how much is rubbing off.

Seattle, Washington
September 7, 1960

Shortly after the start of the 1960 campaign, Vice-President Nixon had to go to the hospital. Mr. Kennedy was asked about this situation at a press conference in Washington, D.C. on September 1, 1960:

QUESTION. Senator, did you say you were not going to discuss the Vice-President until he is out of the hospital?

MR. KENNEDY. That is right.

QUESTION. Does that mean no personal references in your speeches?

MR. KENNEDY. That is right.

QUESTION. But will you resume?

MR. KENNEDY. Well, we will see what happens then. I may discuss some of the Republican shortcomings but not Mr. Nixon's.

QUESTION. You are not going to mention his part in any of them?

MR. KENNEDY. Unless I can praise him.

QUESTION. Do you mean as long as he stays in the hospital he has sanctuary?

MR. KENNEDY. Yes, that is right. I may go there.

I want to express my thanks to all of you, particularly those of you who are college students and can't vote, who came down here anyway. I recognize that the sacrifice is not extensive as I am doing the work this morning and you are not in class. I am glad that you are participating actively in the political process. Artemus Ward, fifty years ago, said, "I am not a politician and my other habits are also good."

Albion, Michigan
October 14, 1960

All along the 1960 campaign trail, Senator Kennedy was recipient of a wide and sometimes amusing variety of gifts from local citizens. The offerings included livestock, food, clothing, and whatever else was available of the local wares. At one stop Kennedy was handed a watermelon weighing 142 pounds. Recoiling in mock horror, Kennedy asked, "Is it still alive?"

QUESTION. Senator, when does the moratorium end on Nixon's hospitalization and your ability to attack him?

MR. KENNEDY. Well, I said I would not mention him unless I could praise him until he got out of the hospital, and I have not mentioned him.

Burbank, California
September 9, 1960

*In September, 1960, Mr. Kennedy went to New York to ac-
cept the Liberal Party nomination for the Presidency:*

I am proud to be the only candidate in 1960 with the
nomination of two political parties, although I am not certain how many tickets are now headed in how many states
by Senator Goldwater.

Just before you met, a weekly news magazine with a wide
circulation featured a section, "Kennedy's Liberal Promises,"
and described me, and I quote, as "the farthest-out Liberal
Democrat around," unquote. While I am not certain of the
beatnik definition of "farthest-out," I am certain that it was
not intended as a compliment.

And last week, as further proof of my credentials, a noted
American clergyman was quoted as saying that our society
may survive in the event of my election, but it certainly
won't be what it was. I would like to think that he was
complimenting me, but I'm not sure he was.

Those of you who are here tonight are proof of the fact
that some of the best friends that Democrats have are not in
the Democratic Party. I think that in November some of
them may be in the Republican Party, but I hold out no
hope at all for the vast and impressive number of Republicans who suddenly, just before election time—those who are
running for office—begin to sound like true Lincolns.

Eight years ago on this occasion, Adlai Stevenson called
this quadrennial outburst of affection "the pause in the real
Republican occupation known as 'The Liberal Hour,'"
and he added, "It should never be confused" (and he was
right) "with any period when Congress is in session."

Mr. Nixon may be very experienced in his kitchen debates. So are a great many other married men I know.

Alexandria, Virginia
August 24, 1960

At a press conference in Des Moines, Iowa, on August 21, 1960, Mr. Kennedy was asked: "What sort of qualifications would you look for in the man you would select for the next Secretary of Agriculture?" He answered:

First, I think he should have been at some part of his life a farmer. Secondly, I think he should live in the midwest United States. Thirdly, he should believe that his responsibility is to preserve the family farm and not liquidate it. Fourth, and finally, it would be helpful if he were a Democrat.

At the 1960 Democratic Convention, both Senator Kennedy and Senator Johnson were active candidates for the Presidential nomination. Prior to the balloting, they both appeared before a joint meeting of the Texas and Massachusetts delegations.

I'm glad we're not going to put these speeches to a vote ... after looking at the Massachusetts and Texas delegates today. Let me just say that I appreciate what Senator Johnson had to say. He made some general references to the shortcomings of other Presidential candidates, but as he was not specific, I assume he was talking about some of the other candidates and not about me. I have found it extremely beneficial serving in the Senate with Senator Johnson as leader. I think if I emerge successfully in the convention, it will be the result of watching Senator Johnson proceed around the Senate for the last eight years. I have learned the lesson well, Lyndon, and I hope it will benefit me in the next twenty-four hours. It is true that Senator Johnson made a wonderful record in answering those quorum calls, and I want to commend him for it. In fact, on every occasion, I said that I thought Senator Johnson should not enter the primaries, that his proper responsibility was as majority leader, and that if he would let Hubert, Wayne, and me settle this matter, we could come to a clear-cut decision.

Prior to the 1960 Democratic Convention, former President Truman said at a press conference that Senator Kennedy was not his first choice for the Democratic Presidential nomination. Senator Kennedy was asked by the press to comment on Mr. Truman's remarks.

The last conversation to which he referred in Independence was less precise than that. He said we must all join together to secure the best man. I did not feel that on that occasion he was asking me to step aside.

In August, 1960, candidate Kennedy was invited to address an AMVET Convention in Miami Beach. However, his schedule did not permit him to appear in person, so he telephoned his address to the Convention.

I should inform you that we are running a small convention of the AMVETs in Detroit this morning, because sitting next to me is the Lieutenant Governor of Michigan, John Swainson, who is an AMVET. Sitting beside me is Pete Koubra who is former National Committeeman of the AMVETs from Michigan, and also Carol Kay, who is the President and Senior Vice-Commander of the AMVETs. So we've got a convention going ourselves.

Texas has sent twenty-one Democratic congressmen to Congress and one Republican—a fair proportion, a good average.

El Paso, Texas
September 12, 1960

We don't want to be like the leader in the French Revolution who said, "There go my people. I must find out where they are going so I can lead them."

* * *

I regret the rain, but it rains, as the Bible tells us, on the just and the unjust alike, on the Republicans as well as Democrats.

Sioux Falls, South Dakota
September 22, 1960

Mr. Chairman, ladies and gentlemen, it is nine in the morning and this will be a quiet, dignified speech.

Philadelphia, Pennsylvania
October 29, 1960

I would like to present to you my three sisters, who have been campaigning around the United States, and who came with us today for the end of the campaign—my sister Eunice Shriver, my sister Jean Smith, and my sister Patricia Lawford. . . . I think Mrs. Lawford got a better hand than the other sisters.

Hartford, Connecticut
November 7, 1960

When I came to Washington to the U.S. Senate, I brought a number of young ladies from Massachusetts to be secretaries. They all got married. Then I got a whole new set of girls and they got married. So if any of you girls feel the prospects are limited in this community you come and work for me.

* * *

Those of you who live in this State of Florida depend upon a moving and expanding country. I know something about the economy of this state. When the rest of the country catches cold, Florida gets pneumonia and Miami is very sick.

Miami, Florida
October 18, 1960

This state knows the issues of this campaign—Senior Citizens. Senator McNamara is chairman of the Senate Committee on Senior Citizens. I am vice-chairman. We are both aging fast.

Warren, Michigan
October 26, 1960

You remember the very old story about a citizen of Boston who heard a Texan talking about the glories of Bowie, Davy Crockett, and all the rest, and finally said, "Haven't you heard of Paul Revere?" To which the Texan answered, "Well, he is the man who ran for help."

Houston, Texas
September 12, 1960

The man in the audience said that I should tell Mr. Nixon that experience is what he will have left after this campaign is over. I don't know why we never think of these things.

New York City
October 27, 1960

On election night, 1960, the Kennedy family and campaign staff waited anxiously as the candidate spoke long-distance with his Vice-Presidential running mate, Lyndon Johnson, in Texas. Finally Kennedy hung up and announced his version of Johnson's conversation: "I hear *you're* losing Ohio, but *we're* doing fine in Pennsylvania."

III

The New Frontier

THE NEW FRONTIER" meant many things to the people of America. It was characterized by a spirit of renewed optimism, determination, and vigor, the qualities of youth so shiningly embodied by President John F. Kennedy. As much as anything else, The New Frontier was an atmosphere, an atmosphere in large part created and reinforced by Kennedy himself and pervading the whole of his administration. Intellect was the raw material of The New Frontier, energy was its driving force, hope its rally cry, and laughter its sound.

With laughter, too, John Kennedy led the way. President Kennedy's wonderful wit was something new to most Americans, and they welcomed it eagerly. Here was a man who could head the most powerful country on earth and still find time to joke and laugh—and to share his laughter with millions.

To many Americans, I am sure, it was this spirit that really brought home the meaning of The New Frontier. And for many, the wit that follows will be the best way of preserving its memory.

President Kennedy's golf game was not the most consistent, but he loved to wager on himself. His system of betting was so complex that only he could understand it, and thus he was able to win most of his matches. However, on one particularly bad day he and his partner, military aide General Chester V. Clifton, had lost most of their bets and came to the 18th green behind by only one stroke. All Clifton had to do was sink a straight four-foot putt to even the match. The General took a long and silent time lining up the shot, and then left the ball two feet short of the cup. Kennedy quietly eyed the ball, then slowly looked up and said, "Nice putt, *Sergeant*."

Comments by President Kennedy at Inaugural Balls in Washington, D.C. on January 20, 1960

I think this is an ideal way to spend an evening and I hope that we can all meet here again tomorrow at one A.M. to do it all over again.

* * *

I don't know a better way to spend an evening—you looking at us and we looking at you.

* * *

The Johnsons and I have been to five balls tonight, and we still have one unfullfilled ambition—and that is to see somebody dance.

John F. Kennedy's sense of humor was occasionally irreverent. He rarely expressed it at the expense of anyone's feelings, but he frequently did make fun of himself. At one Democratic dinner he began his speech with a caustic parody of his own serious and profound Inaugural speech:

We observe tonight not a celebration of freedom but a victory of party. For we have sworn to pay off the same party debt our forebears ran up nearly a year and three months ago. . . . If the Democratic Party cannot be helped by the many who are poor, it cannot be saved by the few who are rich.

When President Kennedy reviewed the Naval and Marine Corps fleet in April, 1962, the sight of the assembled ships was magnificent. Led by the tremendous nuclear-powered carrier, the *Enterprise*, the formation of battleships stretched for miles. The exercises included antisubmarine attacks, and surface-to-air missile demonstrations. The grandeur of the effort, however, was matched by the lack of success during the maneuvers. Missiles rose from the depths of the sea only to weave erratically across the sky and plunge back down again, or fly harmlessly right pass their targets. Later the President remarked acidly, "My God, based on the success of the operation today, I'm sure the word has already gotten to Moscow: 'Come in by sea.' "

The spring day on which President Kennedy was inspecting the nuclear submarine *Thomas A. Edison* turned out to be a raw, windy one. On the pier stood a group of shivering underwater swimmers waiting for inspection. The President tried to make the formality as brief as possible, and upon reaching one sailor who was shivering violently, said, "The Admiral here tells me you fellows don't even feel the cold." The sailor began laughing and Kennedy continued, "Well we're getting right out of here and you fellows can get out of the cold and warm up." The sailor answered immediately, "Mr. President, I'd be happy to stand out here in the cold indefinitely to meet you." Replied Kennedy, "Thanks, but if you don't get out of this cold pretty soon we'll never meet again."

President and Mrs. Kennedy instituted the awarding of a series of honors which they called the Medal of Freedom. In one of the early selections the President favored the artist Ben Shahn, but eventually Andrew Wyeth was chosen. Quipped Kennedy, "Next year, we'll have to go abstract."

Strolling through the White House grounds one day, the President looked admiringly at the revitalized White House Gardens with their lovely petunias and ageratim and commented:

This may go down as the real achievement of this administration.

On a trip to the West Coast, President Kennedy was asked by a little boy, "Mr. President, how did you become a war hero?"

It was absolutely involuntary. They sank my boat.

I don't know whether you realize that this is an historic occasion. We have paid off nearly $4,000,000 that the Kennedy-Johnson ticket ran up in November of 1960. It is now gone forever, which is sad, and all we have left is the Federal deficit.

I suppose a number of things attract us all here today. Some of us think it wise to associate as much as possible with historians and cultivate their good will, though we always have the remedy which Winston Churchill once suggested when he prophesied during World War II that history would deal gently with him. "Because," Mr. Churchill said, "I intend to write it!"

Washington, D.C.
October 3, 1961

Speaking to students at the University of North Carolina after he became President, Mr. Kennedy said that he did not propose to adopt "from the Belgian Constitution a provision giving three votes instead of one to college graduates—at least not until more Democrats go to college."

In a tribute to Senator Warren Magnuson of Washington, President Kennedy listed Magnuson's Senate techniques:

He never visits the Senate until late in the afternoon, when almost everybody has gone home. He comes in at the last minute and waits until he can have the floor, and then he says, "What's my business? Oh, it's nothing important. Just the Grand Coulee Dam!"

Once while speaking of his love of the sea and sailing, President Kennedy told some reporters, "I'd really love to have that yacht Eisenhower laid up in Philadelphia. But he said he did it for economy reasons, and if I took it out of mothballs now they'd never let me hear the end of it."

At a Democratic fund-raising dinner in Miami honoring Senator George A. Smathers of Florida, President Kennedy made these remarks:

Senator Smathers has been one of my most valuable counselors at crucial moments. In 1952 when I was thinking of running for the United States Senate, I went to Senator Smathers and said, "George, what do you think?" He said, "Don't do it, can't win, bad year." [*That was the year Mr. Kennedy won his Senate seat.*]

In 1956, I didn't know whether I should run for vice-president or not so I said, "George, what do you think?" And Senator Smathers replied, "It's your choice!" So I ran and lost.

In 1960 I was wondering whether I ought to run in the West Virginia primary, but the Senator said, "Don't do it. That state you can't possibly carry."

And actually, the only time I really got nervous about the whole matter of Los Angeles was just before the balloting and George came up and said, "I think it looks pretty good for you."

Dave Powers, one of President Kennedy's closest friends and aides, received a scroll from the President on his fiftieth birthday, which read:

President's Special Award, Physical Fitness Program. Walking fifty miles per month from TV to refrigerator and back. Presented to Dave Powers on his fiftieth birthday. In recognition of your athletic ability in hiking to my icebox to drink my Heineken's.

Bob Hope was honored at a dinner in Hollywood on March 4, 1962, for his outstanding work in entertaining American servicemen overseas. One of the highlights of the dinner was the tape-recorded voice of President Kennedy. The President lauded Mr. Hope for his humanitarian efforts and suggested that Mr. Hope consider a Road-to-Washington film.

From my own experience, I can tell him it's not the easiest

road to travel, but it will give him a chance to visit his money—at least what's left of it.

President De Gaulle of France announced early in Mr. Kennedy's term in office that France had developed her own nuclear force so that she could be independent of the United States. A short time after this announcement, the President accepted a loan of the "Mona Lisa" from the French Minister of Culture with these remarks:

Mr. Minister, we in the United States are grateful for this loan from the leading artistic power in the world, France. I must note further that this painting has been kept under careful French control.

And I want to make it clear that, grateful as we are for this painting, we will continue to press ahead with the effort to develop an independent artistic force and power of our own.

President Kennedy was severely criticized by the press for the Bay of Pigs fiasco. Although his staff and advisors had been in favor of his decision, most of those involved were eager to shift the blame onto someone else's shoulders. However, Special Assistant Arthur Schlesinger had been one who had, from the first, informed Kennedy that he was against the plans. When the President was later reminded of this, he replied sarcastically: "Oh sure, Arthur wrote me a memorandum that will look pretty good when he gets around to writing his book on my administration—only he better not publish that memorandum while I'm alive. And I have a title for his book—*Kennedy: The Only Years.*"

John F. Kennedy was not interested in long-winded subjective discussions concerning himself or his office. When asked to express himself on such matters he would reply laconically, "I have a nice home, the office is close by and the pay is good."

Washington is a city of Southern efficiency and Northern charm.

Quoted by William Manchester
in Portrait of a President

The New York Times, *a traditionally Republican newspaper, endorsed John F. Kennedy for the Presidency.*
After his election, the President was quoted as saying:

In part, at least, I am one person who can truthfully say, "I got my job through *The New York Times.*"

At a Washington dinner party shortly after his inauguration, President Kennedy paid tribute to Washington lawyer Clark Clifford who had served as Mr. Kennedy's representative to the Eisenhower administration during the period of transition immediately after Mr. Kennedy's election:

Clark is a wonderful fellow. In a day when so many are seeking a reward to what they contributed to the return of the Democrats to the White House, you don't hear Clark clamoring. He was invaluable to us and all he asked in return was that we advertise his law firm on the backs of one dollar bills.

February, 1961

In 1961 President Kennedy addressed the 39th Annual Convention of the National Association of Broadcasters in Washington, D.C. Honored guests on that occasion were Commander and Mrs. Alan Shepard. Commander Shepard had just completed his historic space flight, to which the President alluded in his opening remarks:

We have with us today the Nation's number one television performer, who, I think, on last Friday morning secured the largest rating of any morning show in recent history.

Barry Goldwater is an excellent photographer. He once took a good picture of President Kennedy and sent it to him for an autograph. The picture came back with this inscription:

For Barry Goldwater, whom I urge to follow the career for which he has shown so much talent—photography. From his friend, John Kennedy.

As President, John F. Kennedy opposed Federal aid to parochial schools. This stand caused much consternation in Catholic circles. Shortly after his education bill was proposed to the Congress, Mr. Kennedy quipped:

As all of you know, some circles invented the myth that after Al Smith's defeat in 1928, he sent a one-word telegram to the Pope: "Unpack."

After my press conference on the school bill, I received a one-word wire from the Pope: "Pack."

One day, early in his administration, President Kennedy went to see the motion picture *Spartacus*. As the film began he spotted his new Secretary of Agriculture Orville Freeman and his wife seated in the row directly ahead of him. The President leaned forward and whispered in Freeman's ear, "Haven't the leaders of the New Frontier got anything better to do with their time than spend it going to the movies?" Kennedy's barb was, however, well matched by Freeman's quick retort, "I wanted to be immediately available on a moment's notice if the President wanted me."

It would be premature to ask your support in the next election and it would be inaccurate to thank you for it in the past.

National Industrial Conference Board
Washington, D.C.
February 13, 1961

On September 27, 1962, President Kennedy addressed a crowd at Wheeling Stadium in Wheeling, West Virginia, the state in which he had defeated the then Senator Hubert Humphrey in his first Presidential primary race. In his opening remarks the President said:

Sometimes when Senator Humphrey and I get together to discuss the crises which pile up on the President's desk, we may wonder which of us you did the greater favor for.

At a Gridiron Club Dinner in Washington a few years after he became President, Mr. Kennedy was in rare form. He used the occasion to comment humorously on the fact that Mr. Adzhubei, Premier Khrushchev's son-in-law, had made an unprecedented visit to Rome:

I have a very grave announcement. The Soviet Union has once again recklessly embarked upon a provocative and extraordinary change in the status quo in an area which they know full well I regard as having a special and historic relationship. I refer to the deliberate and sudden deployment of Mr. Adzhubei to the Vatican.

I am told that this plot was worked out by a group of Khrushchev's advisors who have all been excommunicated from the Church. It is known as Ex-Com.

Reliable refugee reports have also informed us that hundreds of Marxist bibles have been unloaded and are being hidden in caves throughout the Vatican. We will now pursue the contingency plan for protecting the Vatican City which was previously prepared by the National Security Council. The plan is known as Vat 69.

I appreciate very much your generous invitation to be here tonight.

You bear heavy responsibilities these days, and an article I read some time ago reminded me of how particularly heavy the burdens of present-day events bear upon your profession.

You may remember that in 1851, the New York *Herald Tribune,* under the sponsorship of Horace Greeley, included as its London correspondent an obscure journalist by the name of Karl Marx.

We are told that the foreign correspondent, Marx, stone broke and with a family ill and undernourished, constantly appealed to Greeley and managing editor Charles Dana for an increase in his munificent salary of $5 per installment, a salary which he and Engels labeled as the "lousiest petty bourgeois cheating."

But when all his financial appeals were refused, Marx looked around for other means of livelihood and fame, and eventually terminated his relationship with the *Tribune* and devoted his talents full time to the cause that would bequeath to the world the seeds of Leninism, Stalinism, revolution, and the Cold War.

If only this capitalistic New York newspaper had treated him more kindly, if only Marx had remained a foreign correspondent, history might have been different, and I hope all publishers will bear this lesson in mind the next time they receive a poverty-stricken appeal for a small increase in the expense account from an obscure newspaperman.

I have selected as the title of my remarks tonight "The President and the Press." Some may suggest that this would be more naturally worded "The President vs. the Press," but these are not my sentiments tonight.

It is true, however, that when a well-known diplomat from another country demanded recently that our State Department repudiate certain newspaper attacks on his colleague, it was necessary for us to reply that this administration was not responsible for the press, for the press had already made clear that it was not responsible for this administration.

If in the last few months, your White House reporters and photographers have been attending church services with regularity, that has surely done them no harm.

On the other hand, I realize that your staff and wire service photographers may be complaining that they do not enjoy the same green privileges at the local golf courses which they once did. It is true that my predecessor did not object as I do to pictures of one's golfing skill in action. But neither, on the other hand, did he ever bean a Secret Service man.

American Newspaper Publishers Association
April 27, 1961

On June 17, 1963, President Kennedy addressed a luncheon for Sponsors and Editors of Historical Publications at the White House:

I want to welcome all of you and express a very warm appreciation to this combination of unlimited wealth and scholarship. It's a very happy occasion—both groups are happiest when with each other, so that I think it's appropriate that we meet together today.

Speaking of the religious issue, I asked the Chief Justice tonight whether he thought our new education bill was constitutional and he said: "It's clearly constitutional—it hasn't got a prayer."

Gridiron Club
Washington, D.C.

John Kennedy made this interesting observation about the public's "image" of politics:

Mothers may still want their sons to grow up to be President, but, according to a famous Gallup poll of some years ago, some 73 per cent do not want them to become politicians in the process.

In 1963 when a group of Communists hijacked a Venezuelan freighter, the U.S. Navy's response in the ensuing search disappointed President Kennedy. They were slow and ineffective in locating the vessel, and the President finally called the Secretary of the Navy to find out just what the problem was. The Secretary's reply was that the orders had not come through the right channels. A few days later, the Venezuelan President arrived in Washington for a state visit. Elaborate preparation had been made for a magnificent military reception. However, plans were abruptly canceled because of a sudden and very violent rainstorm. An hour later, with wind and rain still at full force, Kennedy looked out his office window and noticed a rain-soaked and bedraggled formation of soldiers still standing in order. He hurriedly called his military aide to find out why, since the ceremony had been canceled, these men were still standing there. He was told once again that their orders had not yet arrived "through channels." After instructing the aide to dismiss the soldiers, Kennedy remarked coldly, "You can see why the Navy has been unable to locate the Venezuelan freighter."

In December, 1960, a short time after the election, the President elect met at the Hotel Carlyle in New York City with one of his advisors, Stewart Udall, to discuss plans for the Inauguration. Mr. Udall suggested that Mr. Kennedy add a touch of culture to the ceremonies by inviting Robert Frost to speak. Said Mr. Kennedy:

Great idea. We'll do it. But with Frost's skill with words, people will remember his speech instead of mine. I think we'd better have him read a poem.

I also regret very much that another honored guest of this dinner on a previous occasion is not with us tonight. I follow his career with more interest than he might imagine. In his quest for the Presidency, Governor Rockefeller follows the examples of other distinguished New Yorkers—Wendell Willkie, Thomas Dewey, Richard Nixon—and I wish him some margin of success.

Protestant Council of New York
November 8, 1963

On a return visit to the White House on November 5, 1961, former President Truman entertained President Kennedy and the assembled dinner guests with a few selections on the piano. President Kennedy was quoted as having made this comment after Mr. Truman finished his piano recital:

Don't say there is no justice in the world. Stalin has been kicked out of Lenin's tomb and President Truman is back in the White House.

"Delicate" subjects were not out of range of John Kennedy's wit. His gentle teasing was often aimed at the Church and its clergy. At one dinner he appeared with an eminent monsignor who was more than slightly rotund. Kennedy remarked that he found it an "inspiration . . . to be here with . . . one of those lean, ascetic clerics who show the effect of constant fast and prayer, and bring the message to us in the flesh."

There is one photograph of little John Kennedy, Jr., that touched the heart of the entire nation. It is of the small lad racing toward his father, reaching up to be caught in his arms. The photograph was taken as President Kennedy deplaned from Air Force One and walked toward his waiting family. When he saw the picture—reproduced in papers across the nation—he smiled and said: "Every mother in the United States is saying 'Isn't it wonderful to see that love between a son and his father, the way that John races to be with his father.' Little do they know that that son would have raced right by his father to get to that helicopter, but his dad stepped into his path and grabbed him."

There is no city in the United States in which I get a warmer welcome and less votes than Columbus, Ohio.

January 6, 1962

I used to work for INS for a short time, although I have never been able to figure out whether UP belongs to INS or INS belongs to UP.

I want to say that I come here not as a stranger, because I have had during my first five months in office the close observation of Mr. Merriman Smith [UPI White House correspondent], who carried other Presidents through difficult periods before, and who is regarded as one of the leading Presidential collectors of our time.

United Press International Dinner
June 9, 1961

On June 8, 1963, President Kennedy spoke at a breakfast with the Democratic State Committeewomen of California in Hollywood, and commented:

Looking at all you ladies and seeing what you have done with some of your distinguished officeholders, I recall an experience of the suffragettes who picketed the White House back during the First World War. The leader of the suffragettes was arrested. And as she was taken away in a truck, she turned to her girls and said, "Don't worry girls. Pray to the Lord. *She* will protect you."

On July 11, 1962, President Kennedy addressed some remarks to a visiting group of American Field Service students at the White House. After speaking for a while, the President introduced Senator Eugene McCarthy of Minnesota, who assured the students that the Congress was sympathetic to the President's "great international ideas and programs and projects." President Kennedy then resumed:

For the privilege of speaking before you Senator McCarthy now owes me at least three votes in the next two months!

I want to close by quoting a distinguished German, Mr. Bismarck, who once said that one third of the students of German universities broke down from overwork, another third broke down from dissipation, and the other third ruled Germany. I don't know which third we have here today, but I'm confident that some future President of the United States will welcome you as President, or perhaps even better, the wife of a President, to the White House, and you'll be able to say to him, "I have been here before."

At a dinner at the White House with friends, President Kennedy jokingly said he doubted that Pope John was all the press pictured him to be. He remarked:

You Protestants are always building him up.

President Kennedy enjoyed teasing his Press Secretary, Pierre Salinger, about certain similarities in their wartime experiences. They were both stationed in the Pacific, and both had received a citation for deeds of heroism. Salinger, however, received his medal for an act committed after the war had ended—helping to swim a line to fourteen sailors who were stranded on a sandpit after their patrol craft had been sunk by a typhoon. Kennedy would remark: "I'll never figure out how you got the same medal I did. After all, I was in action against the enemy when I had to swim for it. All you had to contend with was a little peacetime typhoon!"

I want to say that I have been in on-the-job training for about eleven months and feel that I have some seniority rights.

I am delighted to be here with you and with the Secretary of Labor, Arthur Goldberg. I was up in New York, stressing physical fitness, and in line with that, Arthur went over with a group to Switzerland to climb some of the mountains there. They got up about five and he was in bed. He got up to join them later and when they all came back at four o'clock in the afternoon he didn't come back with them.

So they sent out search parties, and there was not a sign that afternoon and night. The next day the Red Cross went out and around, calling: "Goldberg, Goldberg! It's the Red Cross!" Then this voice came down from the mountain: "I gave at the office!"

Those are the liberties you can take with members of the cabinet.

AFL-CIO Convention
Bal Harbour, Florida
December 7, 1961

A lawyer once wrote to President Kennedy and suggested that his crime-fighting brother, Attorney General Robert Kennedy, would make a better President. Kennedy responded, "I have consulted Bobby about it and, to my dismay, the idea appeals to him."

Let me begin by expressing my appreciation for the very deep honor you have conferred upon me. As General De Gaulle occasionally acknowledges America to be the daughter of Europe, so I am pleased to come to Yale, the daughter of Harvard.

It might be said now that I have the best of both worlds: a Harvard education and a Yale degree.

I am particularly glad to become a Yale man because as I

think about my troubles, I find that a lot of them have come from other Yale men. Among businessmen, I have had a minor disagreement with Roger Blough of the Law School class of 1931 and I have had some complaints too from my friend, Henry Luce, of the class of 1920, not to mention, always, William F. Buckley, Jr., of the class of 1950.

Yale Commencement Address
June 11, 1962

My grandfather always used to claim that the Fitzgeralds were descended from the Geraldinis, who came from Venice. I have never had the courage to make that claim, but I will make it now, on Columbus Day in this State of New Jersey.

Newark, New Jersey
October 12, 1961

I would like to announce at this time that as Commander-in-Chief, I am exercising my privilege of directing the Secretary of the Army and the Superintendent of West Point to remit all existing confinements and other cadet punishments, and I hope it will be possible to carry this out today.

General Westmoreland was slightly pained to hear that this was impending in view of the fact that one cadet, who I am confident will some day be head of the Army, had just been committed for eight months and is about to be released. But I am glad to have this opportunity to participate in the advancement of his military career.

I want to say that I wish all of you the greatest success. While I say that, I am not unmindful of the fact that two graduates of this Academy have reached the White House and neither was a member of my party. Until I am more certain that this trend will be broken, I wish that all of you may be generals and not commanders-in-chief.

West Point Commencement Address
June 7, 1962

This has been a week of momentous events around the world. The long and painful struggle in Algeria came to an end. Both nuclear powers and neutrals labored in Geneva for a solution to the problem of a spiraling arms race, and also to the problems that so vex our relations with the Soviet Union. The Congress opened hearings on a trade bill which is far more than a trade bill, but an opportunity to build a stronger and closer Atlantic Community. And my wife had her first and last ride on an elephant!

University of California
at Berkeley
March 23, 1962

President Kennedy enjoyed joking not only with members of his administrative staff but with his personal White House staff as well. He was very concerned with each step in the renovation of the White House, and would inquire almost daily on its progress. When the rose garden was being redesigned and replanted he would periodically jump up and call out the window to the digging men, "Struck oil yet?"

John F. Kennedy on the farmer:

The farmer is the only man in our economy who buys everything at retail, sells everything he sells at wholesale, and pays the freight both ways.

Visiting Wisconsin, President Kennedy was made honorary chieftain by an Indian tribe. Placing the feather headdress on his head, the President remarked, "Next time I go to the movies to see cowboys and Indians, I'll be with *us*."

President Kennedy, in the very early days of his administration, was always cognizant of the fact that many of the situations he faced were a result of actions of the previous administration. At an early meeting of the National Security Council, President Kennedy opened a folder filled with briefs of problems: "Now, let's see," the President said, "Did we inherit these or are these our own?"

On the same subject, President Kennedy had this to say: "I had plenty of problems when I came in, but wait until the fellow that follows me sees what he will inherit."

There are not so many differences between politics and football. Some Republicans have been unkind enough to suggest that my close election was somewhat similar to the Notre Dame-Syracuse game [won by Notre Dame with a disputed penalty]. But I am like Notre Dame. We just take it as it comes along. We're not giving it back.

Politics is an astonishing profession. It has enabled me to go from being an obscure member of the junior varsity at Harvard to being an honorary member of the Football Hall of Fame.

National Football Foundation Dinner
New York City
December, 1961

In a speech in October, 1961, before 3,500 Democratic precinct workers in Chicago, the President remarked:

I just want to see who did it last November, 1960, and there they are. They said terrible things about you, but I never believed it. I hope you will do the same for Congressman Sid Yates. I understand that Mayor Daley plans to keep you locked up here until November 6th, then turn you loose.

After President Kennedy had nominated John Galbraith as the new United States Ambassador to India, Mr. Kennedy was informed by Mr. Galbraith that the Ambassador-to-be's young son, Peter, was not too anxious to leave all his friends in Boston and move to India. On April 1, 1961, the President sent the following soothing letter to young Peter Galbraith:

Dear Peter:

I learned from your father that you are not anxious to give up your school and friends for India.

I think I know a little bit about how you feel.

More than 20 years ago, our family was similarly uprooted when we went to London where my father was Ambassador.

My younger brother and sisters were about your age. They had, like you, to exchange new friends for old.

For anyone interested, as your father says you are, in animals, India has the most fascinating possibilities. The range is from elephants to cobras, although I gather the cobras have to be handled professionally.

As a P.S. the President added:

I wish a little I were going also.

President Kennedy's fight for the medicare bill was the object of intense criticism from the American Medical Association. On May 20, 1962, Kennedy addressed a large rally of senior citizens at Madison Square Garden, his speech being carried on nationwide television. The following night the AMA responded with a harsh counter-attack. At his next conference Kennedy casually acknowledged, "I read their statement and . . . I gathered they were opposed to it."

Prior to his becoming President, John F. Kennedy was a member of the Harvard Board of Overseers. On January 9, 1961, Kennedy attended his last meeting as a member of the Board immediately after his election. As he entered University Hall to attend that last meeting, he was met by cheering students. The new President turned to the students and said:

I am here to go over your grades with Dr. Pusey and I'll protect your interests.

Each year the wives of United States Senators and Congressmen give a breakfast in honor of the President's wife. However, the 1962 affair found Jacqueline Kennedy very close to childbirth, making it necessary that her husband take her place as guest of honor. The President very graciously did so, and told the assembled ladies:

I am very glad to be here today representing in a very second-rate way a substitute for my wife, who is engaged in increasing the gross national product in her own way. The most significant guest at our dinner for the Grand Duchess the other night was not the Grand Duchess or the Duke or the Chief Justice, but Dr. Spock, who was standing by!

> *International Inn*
> *Washington, D.C.*
> *May 2, 1963*

President Kennedy held a meeting in the White House in November, 1961, for fifteen of the top Army commanders from around the world who had returned to Washington for a Pentagon briefing. As the President gazed at the Army brass surrounding him, he joked:

I realize that it is entirely a coincidence that this meeting occurred at the time of the Army-Navy game.

In January, 1963, President Kennedy was hard at work on his economic message for Congress, which was to answer critics of his economic program. He glanced up from his papers at Walter Heller, bleary-eyed and exhausted from long days and nights of work on the message. "Walter," the President said, "I want to make it perfectly clear that I resent these attacks on you."

I think this is the most extraordinary collection of talent, of human knowledge, that has ever been gathered together at the White House—with the possible exception of when Thomas Jefferson dined alone.

> *White House Dinner Honoring Nobel Prize Winners*

Shortly after he became President, Mr. Kennedy asked Professor James Tobin of Yale University to come to Washington as a member of his Council of Economic Advisors.

"I'm just an Ivory Tower economist," Mr. Tobin told the President. Mr. Kennedy replied:

That's the best kind. As a matter of fact, I'm an Ivory Tower President.

In 1962 President Kennedy addressed the members of the President's Commission on the Status of Women, and began:

I want to express my thanks to all of you for an important assignment. We have established this Commission for two reasons. One is for my own self-protection: every two or three weeks Mrs. May Craig asks me what I am doing for women!

A year after his highly publicized dispute with the steel industry, President Kennedy could still reflect upon it with a touch of humor. While speaking at a New York dinner he commented on the fact that at that same moment, in the very same hotel, ex-President Eisenhower was accepting an award as the person who had done the most for the steel industry that year. Said Kennedy: "Last year *I* won the award . . . they came to Washington to present it to me, but the Secret Service wouldn't let them in."

One of President Kennedy's White House aides was described in the newspapers as "corruscatingly" brilliant. "Those guys should never forget," observed the President wryly, "50,000 votes the other way and we'd all be corruscatingly stupid."

On May 1, 1961, in a note to Arthur Hays Sulzberger, Chairman of the Board of The New York Times, *Mr. Kennedy had this to say concerning Mr. Sulzberger's recent acquisition of a new rocking chair:*

You will recall what Senator Dirksen said about the rocking chair—it gives you a sense of motion without any sense of danger.

Told by one of his aides in August, 1961, that the millionth tourist during his term of office was about to go through the White House, Mr. Kennedy joked:

Will he be a Cuban or a freedom rider or a woman in shorts?

President Kennedy admired former President Harry Truman, and each year faithfully telephoned him on his birthday. On May 8, 1963, Truman's 79th birthday, President Kennedy called him in Kansas City, Mo., and quipped:

I must say that I share the view of the country that you can't be 79 when you can out-walk Bobby and out-talk Hubert. I think we can look for a lot more good years.

I recognize tonight that I bear a heavy responsibility of having kept a distinguished group of Americans who paid $125 for this dinner from that dinner for an hour and thirty minutes.

But, I wish to say that—if I may quote an old East Side expression—what you have lost on bananas, you are going to make up on the apples, because this could have been one of the longest dinners in the history of these occasions.

Lyndon [Johnson] is good for forty-five minutes, when he is given a chance; Ambassador Stevenson has been known to go for a very long time; Frank Pace has a very long story to tell; and Bob Hope, will, if called upon. So this might have gone to one or two in the morning but, because of my imminent journey to Paris, you'll be out—hungry, rather unhappy —but you will be home early tonight.

It is now one-thirty in Paris and I am due there at ten-thirty, and I do not believe it would be a good start to keep the General waiting. So I shall be brief. . . .

Eleanor Roosevelt Cancer Foundation Dinner
New York City
May 30, 1961

In his address to the 1961 graduating class of the Naval Academy at Annapolis, President Kennedy stated:

In the past I have had some slight contact with this service, though I never did reach the state of professional and physical perfection where I could hope that anyone would ever mistake me for an Annapolis graduate. . . . I know you are constantly warned . . . not to mix . . . in politics. I should point out however . . . that my rapid rise from a reserve lieutenant of uncertain standing to Commander-in-Chief has been because I did not follow that very good advice.

President Kennedy, a voracious newspaper reader who was particularly sensitive to editorial appraisals, once quipped: "I'd rather be Fleesonized than Krocked."

During the Kennedy administration the White House became a meeting place for creative and literary notables. Jacqueline Kennedy hoped that both the office and the home of the President would attract and stimulate people from all the creative arts. Quipped the President about the White House: ". . . it's becoming a sort of eating place for artists. But *they* never ask *us* out."

John F. Kennedy could appreciate style, grace, and "class" wherever they were found. During the 1961 Berlin crisis he received a letter from France's President De Gaulle, who urged Kennedy not to negotiate. De Gaulle had phrased his argument beautifully, with a literate and graceful use of metaphor. President Kennedy became so excited over the elegance of the letter that he read it aloud to three of his friends. "Isn't that beautiful?" he asked them at the end. "You agree with it?" asked one of the listeners, incredulously. "Oh, no!" exclaimed Kennedy quickly. "But what a marvelous style!"

Those of you who regard my profession of political life with some disdain should remember that it made it possible for me to move from being an obscure lieutenant in the United States Navy to Commander-in-Chief in fourteen years with very little technical competence.

University of North Carolina
October 12, 1961

In his remarks at an Evening Parade following an inspection of the Marine Barracks in 1962, President Kennedy commented:

I was invited a month ago by General [David M.] Shoup to come here to see whether the instructions given by President Thomas Jefferson to Colonel Burrows in regard to constructing a barracks here which would be near to the Navy Yard and also, in his phrase, "within easy marching distance of Washington," had been carried out.

I also, to my dismay, learned that one more impressive Washington title did not have as much significance as I'd thought. I had always enjoyed the title of Commander-in-Chief until I was informed by General Shoup tonight that the Marines who are here, and others like them in this area and many others, can be moved around at his command; that the only forces that cannot be transferred from Washington without my express permission are members of the Marine Corps Band. They are the only forces that I have. But I want it announced that we propose to hold the White House against all odds at least for some time to come, and we are determined to maintain the spirit which you have shown tonight.

July 12, 1962

On November 29, 1962, President John Kennedy addressed a national closed-circuit television audience on a broadcast which opened a $30 million fund-raising campaign on behalf of the National Cultural Center. During his remarks the President commented:

I want to assure the officials of my administration tonight that this demonstration of support for the arts is modest and painless compared to what has been required of past governments and past administrations.

In 1664, Louis XIV, in his own efforts to encourage the arts, donned brilliant tights and played in a drama called "Furious Roland" before a happy court. Moreover, he drafted the highest officers of his administration for the play so that, according to an account, all clad in brilliant tights themselves, they passed before the Queen and the court.

This was suggested tonight but for some reason or other the committee turned it down. But we are glad to be here in any case.

National Guard Armory
Washington, D.C.

Chairman Khrushchev has compared the United States to a worn-out runner living on its past performance and stated that the Soviet Union would out-produce the United States by 1970.

Without wishing to trade hyperbole with the Chairman, I do suggest that he reminds me of the tiger hunter who had picked a place on the wall to hang the tiger's skin long before he caught the tiger. This tiger has other ideas. We invite the U.S.S.R. to engage in this competition which is peaceful and which could only result in a better living standard for both our people.

In short, the United States is not such an aged runner and, to paraphrase Mr. Coolidge, "We *do* choose to run."

Summer 1961

One afternoon John Kennedy had appointments with two of his speech writers. Each had arrived with a draft in hand. Because he was behind schedule, Kennedy spoke to them both at once—and, scanning both drafts, decided he liked certain portions of each. To the consternation of both writers he announced, "Weave them together." As each started to protest that they were two distinct speeches, the President started walking out the door, interrupting them with, "Just go out and write it up and have a new draft here by five o'clock. This reminds me of my father. When someone gave him an idea or a memorandum, he would say 'This is lousy. It's no good.' Then they would ask what he wanted and he would say, 'That's up to you' and walk out of the room. That's what *I* am doing now!"

President Kennedy was a man whose innate vitality was not long subdued in tedious conversations. One day, during such a discussion he suddenly rose from his desk, picked up his cane, and started practicing golf swings. He looked up, laughed, and said "I'm getting to be more like Ike every day!"

When in the company of old and close friends, John F. Kennedy enjoyed teasing them about the prestige of the office of the Presidency. One evening, the President and his Under Secretary of the Navy, Paul Fay, sat down to play a game of checkers—with the checkerboard supported on their knees. Fay was winning the first game when suddenly Kennedy began coughing violently. The checkerboard bounced off, spilling all the checkers onto the floor. Commented Kennedy: "One of those unfortunate incidents of life, Redhead." He then added, "We'll never really know if the Under Secretary was going to strategically outmaneuver the Commander-in-Chief." They began the game again—but this time Kennedy's memory had been refreshed on the strategy of a game he had not played in a long while. The President was victorious.

On November 2, 1961, in a campaign speech for Richard J. Hughes in his race for the New Jersey governorship against former Secretary of Labor James P. Mitchell, President Kennedy had this to say:

One year ago at this time I came to this city around dark after having made about fifteen speeches. In the last nine months I'm happy to say this is the first stump speech I've made for a candidate and I'm glad it's here in New Jersey.

I am somewhat out of practice. But I will say that the last time I came to New Jersey it was just after Mr. Nixon had turned down the fifth debate. And I gather that Mr. Mitchell feels that no Republican should ever be caught in debate again.

The day before Paul ("Red") Fay, Kennedy's old wartime friend, was to be sworn in as Under Secretary of the Navy, he and his family were forced to crash-land while on a flight in a Navy plane. The near disaster made front-page news across the country. At the swearing-in ceremony the President quipped, "I never knew a fellow who went to such lengths to get publicity for a little ceremony like this!"

Secretary of Labor Arthur Goldberg was credited with averting a strike at the Metropolitan Opera during 1961. President Kennedy paid notice to Mr. Goldberg's efforts at a Washington dinner party on September 25, 1961, where the entertainment included Metropolitan Opera stars Roberta Peters and Jerome Hines. In introducing the opera stars to the audience, the President remarked:

The singers have appeared here under the sponsorship of Arthur Goldberg.

Despite the disaster of the Bay of Pigs invasion, a Gallup Poll taken shortly after revealed that the President's popularity was higher than ever and that he registered favorably with eighty-three percent of those interviewed.

In April, 1961, upon learning this news, Mr. Kennedy exclaimed:

My God, it's as bad as Eisenhower.

During President Kennedy's first day in the White House, he noted that his personal secretary, Evelyn Lincoln had his reading copy of his Inaugural Address lying on her desk. He told her, "I read the other day that one of the former Presidents was offered $75,000 for his Inaugural Address. Mrs. Lincoln, give me a pen so I can sign mine." Having signed it, he added, "Here—keep this $75,000 for me!"

For all that I have been reading in the last three, four, or five months about the great conservative revival sweeping the United States, I thought perhaps no one was going to show up today.

Young Democrats Convention
Miami Beach, Florida
December, 1961

Theodore C. Sorensen was a key Kennedy aide and chief speechwriter for the President. Rarely did Mr. Sorensen make any speeches of his own. However, Mr. Sorensen did make one speech in Nebraska in which he criticized their educational system. This speech had many Nebraskans up in arms. When asked about the predicament that Mr. Sorensen found himself in, Mr. Kennedy remarked in July, 1961:

That's what happens when you let a speechwriter out on his own.

On July 2, 1961, President Kennedy enlivened a ceremony for the signing of a housing bill with a touch of Shakespeare.

Noting the absence of two Alabama Democrats, Representative Albert Rains and Senator John J. Sparkman, who had maneuvered the bill through Congress, the President declared:

Having this bill signed without them here is somewhat like having *Hamlet* played without the Prince.

Merriman Smith has covered the White House for United Press for many years and is considered the dean of White House reporters. In January, 1961, at a White House party for newsmen after his Inauguration, President Kennedy took Mr. Smith over to meet Mrs. Kennedy. His introduction went like this:

I want you to meet Merriman Smith. We inherited him with the White House.

Early in the fall of 1962 Kennedy went to Wheeling, West Virginia. As President Kennedy's motorcade moved down the streets of Wheeling, he spotted a group of hospital nurses standing on the sidewalk. He asked the driver to stop so that he could shake their hands. The following morning he received a wire from them which said, "Thank you so much for stopping. God bless you. Sincerely, Wheeling Hospital Student Nurses." The President promptly sent a wire back which read: "If we are ever sick we are coming to the Wheeling General Hospital." He had it signed, "White House Staff."

On June 9, 1962, President Kennedy attended a fund-raising dinner honoring Matthew McClosky on his appointment as Ambassador to Ireland. During his speech the President remarked:

I also want to commend this idea of the $250 dinner. This is like that story of the award of prizes by the Moscow Cultural Center, the first prize being one week in Kiev and the second prize being two weeks. For $100 you get speeches; for $250 you don't get any speeches. You can't get bargains like that any more!

Mayflower Hotel
Washington, D.C.

During John Kennedy's administration there was a strong faction among liberal intellectuals that viewed the President with deep suspicion. When Kennedy learned that the leader of this faction was going to write an article about him for *The American Scholar*, it was arranged that they have lunch together. The luncheon discussion was lively and the talk covered a wide range of subjects—including a discussion of the role of the writer in America. After the seemingly pleasant meeting, the author proceeded to write a highly critical article. Commented Kennedy when he read it: "We wined him and dined him, and talked about Hemingway and Dreiser with him, and I later told Jackie what a good time she missed, and then he went away and wrote that piece!"

The last time that I came to this stadium was twenty-two years ago, when I visited it in November of 1940 as a student at a near-by small school for the game with Stanford. I must say, I had a much warmer reception today than I did on that occasion. In those days, we used to fill these universities for football, and now we do it for academic events, and I'm not sure that this doesn't represent a rather dangerous trend for the future of our country.

University of California
March 23, 1962

It has recently been suggested that whether I serve one or two terms in the Presidency, I will find myself at the end of that period at what might be called the awkward age, too old to begin a new career and too young to write my memoirs.

National Industrial Conference Board
Washington, D.C.
February 13, 1961

In November, 1963—on one of his last weekends—the President and his wife visited their newly built home in Virginia. While outdoors, he was being photographed by the visiting White House reporter. Mrs. Kennedy handed her husband some lumps of sugar to feed their pet pony, but after giving them to the pet the President was surprised to find the animal nibbling at him. Trying unsuccesfully to ease himself free, Kennedy turned to the photographer and laughed, "Keep shooting. You're about to watch a President being eaten by a horse."

Poet Robert Frost was honored by Congress' awarding to him the Congressional Medal in recognition of his contributions to American letters. On March 25, 1961, presenting the medal to Mr. Frost at the White House, President Kennedy said that he supposed that the poet was disappointed that it was not a more controversial decision by Congress in voting the medal for Mr. Frost but a unanimous one. The President went on to say:

It's the only thing they've been able to agree on for a long time.

President Kennedy was warmly greeted when he addressed the convention of the United Auto Workers in 1962, and opened his speech by quipping:

Last week, after speaking to the Chamber of Commerce and the president of the American Medical Association, I began to wonder how I got elected. And now I remember.

I said last week to the Chamber that I thought I was the second choice for President of a majority of the members of the Chamber; anyone else was first choice.

Convention Hall
Atlantic City, N.J.
May 8, 1962

President Kennedy's relationship with the press teetered back and forth between mild antagonism and real comradship. But whatever the mood of the moment, the relationship was never dull. Once, after Kennedy had been in the constant company of a certain head of state for two days, a slightly puzzled reporter cornered Press Secretary Pierre Salinger about a somewhat ambiguous statement Kennedy had made during that time. Salinger reported back, "The President said to tell you he doesn't know what he meant. He said that is just the way he gets after two days with so-and-so!"

When we got into office, the thing that surprised me most was to find that things were just as bad as we'd been saying they were.
Dinner Honoring President Kennedy's 44th Birthday
Washington, D.C.
May 27, 1961

The President made this response to a group of women delegates to the United Nations who had suggested at a White House function that someday there might be a woman President:

I want to say that I had not expected that the standard of revolt would be raised in the Royal Pavilion here, but I'm always rather nervous about how you talk about women who are active in politics, whether they want to be talked about as women or as politicians.

Unable to attend a testimonial luncheon in honor of the then Postmaster General Edward Day in Springfield, Illinois, President Kennedy sent this telegram:

I am delighted to learn of the testimonial luncheon. I know that the Postmaster General will enjoy his day off in Springfield, and I am only sorry that I cannot join in this tribute.

I am sending this message by wire, since I want to be certain that this message reaches you in the right place and at the right time.

President Kennedy's wit could often mask a serious reaction. Once, when being interviewed by a *Look* Magazine reporter, he was asked a question concerning a vicious rumor currently in circulation. His only reply was, "You print that story and I just might wind up owning *Look* Magazine."

This is a double birthday party today. The Children's Bureau is fifty years old and so is Secretary Ribicoff. This is an awkward birthday for the Secretary, because he is too young to retire and too old to be President.

Fiftieth Anniversary
of the United States Children's Bureau
Washington, D.C.
April 8, 1962

In a Washington ceremony on May 8, 1961, President Kennedy introduced Astronaut Alan Shepard, Jr.:

We have with us today the nation's number one television performer, who I think on last Friday morning secured the largest rating of any morning show in recent history.

And I think it does credit to him that he is associated with such a distinguished group of Americans whom we are all glad to honor today—his companions in the flight to outer space—so I think we'll give them all a hand. They are the tanned and healthy ones; the others are Washington employees.

I also want to pay a particular tribute to some of the people who worked in this flight: Robert Gilruth, who was director of the Space Task Force Group at Langley Field; Walter Williams, the operations director of Project Mercury; the NASA Deputy Administrator, Dr. Hugh Dryden; Lieutenant Colonel Glenn, Jr.; and, of course, Jim Webb, who is head of NASA.

Most of these names are unfamiliar. If the flight had not been an overwhelming success, these names would be very familiar to everyone.

A dilemma, it seems to me, is posed by the occasion of a Presidential address to a business group on business conditions less than four weeks after entering the White House, for it is too early to be claiming credit for the new administration and too late to be blaming the old one.

National Industrial Conference Board
Washington, D.C.
February 13, 1961

My experience in government is that when things are non-controversial, beautifully coordinated, and all the rest, it must be that there is not much going on.

While reading an intelligence report from the Central Intelligence Agency, Presidential aide Major General Chester V. Clifton came across the word "Draconian." Puzzled by its meaning, he looked it up and then carefully noted its definition in the margin: "cruel, inhuman!" President Kennedy then read the report, but coming to the word, he stopped and asked, "Who put this in here?" Clifton answered, "I did." Kennedy needled him, "That's the trouble with you military; now if you'd had a classic Harvard education, you would have known what the word meant."

A few days later, the President was once again reading a CIA intelligence report and he came across a very technical military term, "permissive link." Kennedy asked Clifton, "Well, what's this mean?" After explaining it to him, Clifton continued, "Mr. President, if you'd had a classic military education at West Point, you would have known what the word was." Kennedy could not help laughing and adding an admiring, "Touché."

Whenever he addressed a meeting of the National Association of Manufacturers, President Kennedy was cognizant of the fact that he was not speaking before the friendliest of audiences. Mr. Kennedy opened an address to the NAM in December, 1961, with these remarks:

I understand that President McKinley and I are the only two Presidents of the United States ever to address such an occasion. I suppose that President McKinley and I are the only two that are regarded as fiscally sound enough to be qualified for admission to this organization on an occasion such as this.

In Georgetown, speaking of the Presidency just before his Inauguration, Mr. Kennedy commented:

It's a big job. It isn't going to be so bad. You've got time to think. You don't have all those people bothering you that you had in the Senate—besides, the pay is pretty good.

Special ceremonies were held at the White House in November, 1691 in honor of the 46th biennial general assembly of the Union of American Hebrew Congregations. At these ceremonies President Kennedy received a gift of a sacred Torah. In accepting the Torah, the President turned to the then Secretary of Labor, Arthur Goldberg, who is a trustee of the Union of American Hebrew Congregations, and said:

I'll ask the Secretary of Labor to translate this for me.

Professor Arthur Holcombe, one of President Kennedy's Harvard mentors was once a visitor at the White House with a small group of dignitaries. Upon recognizing his former instructor, President Kennedy jibed, "Professor, I understand that you always vote for your former students when they are running for office. What do you do when two of your former students run for the same office at the same time?" It was immediately apparent that Kennedy was referring to the 1952 senatorial campaign between himself and Henry Cabot Lodge, also a former Holcombe student. The professor, not wanting to commit himself and feeling at a loss for words said, "Well, I figure out which one of the two will be taken care of by the next administration, and then I vote for the other one." During the laughter that followed, Kennedy whispered to the professor, "I hope that the voters of Massachusetts don't follow your formula next fall when my younger brother is running for the Senate!"

Some years ago, in the city of Fall River, Massachusetts, the mayor was elected by one vote, and every time he went down the street, everyone would come up to him and say, "Say, Dan, I put you in office."

And I feel a little like that in Chicago tonight. If all of you had voted the other way—there's about fifty-five hundred of you here tonight—I wouldn't be President of the United States.

Chicago, Illinois

At a Sunday night reception in January, 1961, for his new administration appointees at the White House, Mr. Kennedy remarked to his guests:

The reason for this reception is my desire to see some of the names I have been reading about in the newspaper.

I am delighted that John Bailey's going to take over this job [Chairman of the Democratic National Committee]. He is more popular today than he will be any time again in his life. I will feel that he is doing a good job when you all say, "Well, Kennedy is all right, but Bailey's the one who is really making the mistakes."

John F. Kennedy's biographers often note that, although he took life and his work seriously, he never took himself too seriously. Many of his friends enjoy recounting the numerous times when Kennedy did his work and conducted conversations while soaking in the bathtub. One day a friend walked in to speak to him and Kennedy was reading, as usual, in deep hot water. Around him floated some of his son John-John's plastic toys. He glanced up, looked around at the water, and smiling, said, "What would people think if they could see the President of the United States in his bathtub—with these *ducks?*"

At a White House ceremony honoring submarine and Artic research scientist Waldo K. Lyon on August 7, 1962, President Kennedy quipped:

Those of us who have difficulty navigating at sea are astonished at the ability to navigate under ice.

Last year, more Americans went to symphonies than went to baseball games. This may be viewed as an alarming statistic, but I think that both baseball and the country will endure.

White House Youth Concert
August 6, 1962

It's a vital business, the running of a democracy, and it's important that all of us register and vote for the party of our choice.

I am supporting the party of my choice and I intend to vote in the November elections.

Washington, D.C.
August 28, 1962

When David Dubinsky, president of the International Ladies Garment Workers Union, visited the White House for dinner, President Kennedy pointed out to him a photo showing Kennedy receiving a Torah from Dr. Maurice

Eisendrath, president of the Union of American Hebrew Congregations. Dubinsky looked at the picture and asked, "Why didn't you wear a hat?"

Responded Kennedy with a smile, "Because I'm Reform."

I feel honored to join you at this distinguished university.

In the year 1717, King George I of England donated a very valuable library to Cambridge University and at very nearly the same time, had occasion to dispatch a regiment to Oxford.

The King, remarked one famous wit, had judiciously observed the condition of both universities—one was a learned body in need of loyalty and the other was a loyal body in need of learning.

I am deeply honored by the degree which you awarded me today and I think it is appropriate to speak at this university for both loyalty and learning.

University of Maine
October 19, 1963

The only other President to have visited Ashland was Calvin Coolidge, who never said a word. I was here for only one night and spoke all the time.

Ashland, Wisconsin
September 24, 1963

President Kennedy was in rare form when he addressed a White House correspondents' dinner in 1962, shortly after his famous clash with the steel industry over the increase in the price of steel. The increase was eventually canceled, but only after the President went on national television to bring his case to the people. In his speech before the correspondents, he satirized his own television address:

I have a few opening announcements. First, the sudden and arbitrary action of the officers of this organization in increasing the price of dinner tickets by two dollars and fifty cents over last year constitutes a wholly unjustifiable defiance of the public interest. If this increase is not rescinded but is imitated by the Gridiron, Radio-TV, and other dinners, it will have a serious impact on the entire economy of this city. In this serious hour in our nation's history, when newsmen are awakened in the middle of the night to be given a front page story, when expense accounts are being scrutinized by the Congress, when correspondents are required to leave their families for long and lonely weekends at Palm Beach, the American people will find it hard to accept this ruthless decision made by a tiny handful of executives whose only interest is the pursuit of pleasure. I am hopeful that the Women's Press Club will not join this price rise and will thereby force a rescission.

I'm sure I speak on behalf of all of us in expressing our thanks and very best wishes to Benny Goodman and his group, Gwen Verdon, Miss Sally Ann Howes, and Peter Sellers. I have arranged for them to appear next week on the United States Steel Hour. Actually, I didn't do it. Bobby did it.

President Kennedy's correspondence often contained touches of his ready wit. One day he received a wry letter from newspaper columnist Leonard Lyons, in which Lyons told him the current prices for signed portrait photos of Presidents, past and present: George Washington—$175; Franklin D. Roosevelt—$75; U.S. Grant—$55; John F. Kennedy—$65. Kennedy promptly wrote back:

Dear Leonard:

I appreciate your letter about the market on Kennedy signatures. It is hard to believe that the going price is so high now. In order not to depress the market any further, I will not sign this letter.

In September, 1963, at the Salt Lake City, Utah, airport, President Kennedy pulled the switch to activate generators at the Green River in the Colorado River basin 150 miles away.

I never know when I press these whether I am going to blow up Massachusetts or start the project.

* * *

Then the President listened intently to the loudspeaker for the voice that was supposed to announce the successful starting of the generators.

If we don't hear from him, it's back to the drawing boards.

Like members of Congress, I have been, during the last few days over the Easter holiday, back in touch with my constituents and seeing how they felt and, frankly, I have come back to Washington from Palm Beach and I'm against my entire program.

Washington, D.C.

President Kennedy had not been a resident in the White House long when he received the following telegram. It was sent by Edward Myers of Maine's Saltwater Farms—well-known for their lobsters:

MAY CRAIG SAYS THAT [MAINE SENATOR] ED MUSKIE SAYS THAT YOU SAY WHITE HOUSE SUFFERING ACUTE SHORTAGE MAINE LOBSTERS. WE ARE OPPOSED TO DEPRESSED AREAS WHEREVER LOCATED. HAVE THEREFORE SHIPPED THIS MORNING RAILWAY EXPRESS SIXTEEN LIVE LOBSTERS IN BUSY EXECUTIVE SIZE SMALL ENOUGH TO EAT ONE-HANDED; BIG ENOUGH TO SATISFY UNDERSTANDABLE CRAVING. ASK NOT WHAT YOU CAN DO FOR MAINE RATHER WHAT MAINE CAN DO FOR YOU.

Soon afterward, Mr. Myers received the following letter from the President:

MAINE LOBSTERS ARRIVED IN FINE FETTLE. MY SINCERE THANKS FOR YOUR PROMPT ACTION TO ALLEVIATE LOCAL DISTRESS. HAVING NOW CONSUMED SEVERAL, I AM CONFIDENT THAT AN EQUITABLE SOLUTION COULD BE FOUND FOR ANY PROBLEMS OF SURPLUSES EVER FACED BY SALTWATER FARMS.

Karl Marx used to write for the *Herald Tribune*, but that isn't why I canceled my subscription.

November 18, 1962

Last week, after speaking to the Chamber of Commerce and the AMA, I began to wonder how I got elected and now I remember. . . .

I flew longer—and this will go down in the history books —I flew longer in a helicopter than any President of the United States to come here today. That's the kind of forward-looking administration we have.

United Auto Workers Convention
Atlantic City, New Jersey
May 8, 1962

I am very proud to be here tonight. I'm particularly interested in the fact that two of our distinguished guests are former prime ministers of Peru and are now publishers of newspapers.

It does suggest to those who hold office that when the time comes that if, as they say in the United States, if you can't beat them, join them.

Inter-American Press Association
Miami Beach, Florida
November 18, 1963

Alluding to the fact that his Vice-President, Lyndon Johnson, was quite sensitive, John Kennedy once remarked that writing a birthday telegram to him was like "drafting a state document."

I spoke a year ago today at the Inaugural and I would like to paraphrase a couple of statements I made that day by saying that we observe tonight not a celebration of freedom but a victory of party, for we have sworn to pay off the same party debt our forebears ran up nearly a year and three months ago. Our deficit will not be paid off in the next hundred days, nor will it be paid off in the first one thousand days, nor in the life of this administration, or perhaps even in our lifetime on this planet—but let us begin, remembering that generosity is not a sign of weakness and that ambassadors are always subject to Senate confirmation.

For if the Democratic Party cannot be helped by the many who are poor, it cannot be saved by the few who are rich. So let us begin.

Democratic Fund-Raising Dinner
January, 1962

Greeting students who had been learning about government as participants in the Senate youth program, on February 1, 1963, President Kennedy expressed the hope that one of the young men in the group would one day occupy the White House—but not right away!

The other day I read in a newspaper where Senator Goldwater asked for labor's support before 2,000 cheering Illinois businessmen. . . .

Three years ago and one week, by a landslide, the people of the United States elected me to the Presidency of this country.

AFL-CIO Convention
New York City
November 15, 1963

On June 21, 1962, while speaking to students working in Washington, the President remarked:

Sometimes I wish I just had a summer job here.

I have not always considered the membership of the NAM as among my strongest supporters. I'm not sure you have all approached the New Frontier with the greatest possible enthusiasm and I was, therefore, somewhat nervous about accepting this invitation until I did some studying of the history of this organization. I learned that this organization denounced, on one occasion, and I'll quote, "swollen bureaucracy as among the triumphs of Karl Marx" and decried on another occasion new governmental "paternalism and socialism." I was comforted when reading this very familiar language to note that I was in very good company. For the first attack I quoted was on Calvin Coolidge and the second on Herbert Hoover. I remind you of this only to indicate the happy failure of many of our most pessimistic predictions.

National Association of Manufacturers Convention
December, 1961

At a Washington dinner honoring Matthew McClosky, former Democratic National Treasurer, at the Mayflower Hotel on June 10, 1962, President Kennedy quipped:

I used to wonder when I was in the House how President Truman got into so much trouble. Now I'm beginning to get the idea. . . .

I'm sorry to see Matt go. He's the only businessman we have left.

Waterbury is the easiest city to get crowds or it has the best Democrats in the United States.

Waterbury, Connecticut
October 11, 1962

I want to express my pleasure at this invitation as one whose work and continuity of employment has depended in part upon the union movement.

AFL-CIO Convention
Bal Harbour, Florida
December, 1961

I want to express my appreciation for becoming an instant graduate of this academy and I consider it an honor.

I congratulate you all, and most of all, I congratulate your mothers and fathers who made it possible.

United State Air Force Academy
Graduation Exercises in Colorado Springs
June 5, 1963

I want to register an official protest with the International Ladies' Garment Workers of the sweatshop conditions under which we are working today. I'm not sure that this represents fifty years of progress. It is true that your distinguished President [David Dubinsky] invited me to come to speak on November 3rd as we were heading to a meeting which he was sponsoring three days before election. I would have agreed to anything.

I.L.G.W.U. Housing Project
New York City
May 19, 1962

One Las Vegas gambler is supposed to have said he hoped we'd be as tough on Berlin as we've been on Las Vegas. Well, we intend to be.

U.S. Attorneys Meeting
White House
October 10, 1962

In his remarks at a Birthday Dinner for Governor DiSalle of Ohio in 1962, President Kennedy began:

A hundred years ago, Abraham Lincoln stayed up all one night in a telegraph office, watching the results of an essential gubernatorial contest in this State, in the darkest days of the Civil War. And at the end of the night when the Unionist candidate who supported Lincoln's policies had finally emerged the victor, Lincoln wired, "Glory to God in the highest, Ohio has saved the nation."

Two years ago yesterday, when Governor DiSalle was kind enough to endorse my candidacy, I had somewhat similar sentiments about Ohio.

Columbus, Ohio
January 6, 1962

IV

John F. Kennedy
and the World Leaders

PRESIDENT KENNEDY'S ability to put people at ease with a humorous quip served him well in his meetings with foreign dignitaries and heads of state. His wit made many a state visit more enjoyable, and quite probably more profitable.

But very often John Kennedy's probing wit could be double-edged, both funny and to the point. For instance, when Kennedy met with Soviet Premier Khrushchev in 1961, he noticed a medal on the Premier's chest, and asked what it was. Khrushchev answered that it was the Lenin Peace Prize. "I hope you keep it," said Kennedy.

No doubt, the humorous exchanges both men shared enabled them to get to know each other better. And by understanding Nikita Khrushchev the man, Kennedy was better enabled to deal with Premier Khrushchev the Soviet leader.

The quips and quotes in this next section demonstrate that even in the presence of the most eminent men of his day, John Kennedy retained his remarkable wit and charm.

When the then Soviet Premier Khrushchev and President Kennedy met in the summer of 1961, they spent much of their time conversing about agriculture. Krhushchev seemed to have an obsession with this particular subject. He listened with great interest during one luncheon as Secretary Rusk told him of a new fast-growing American corn that could produce two or more crops a year in the same field. Replied Khrushchev, "Remarkable, but do you know that we have found a way to make vodka from natural gas?" He looked at President Kennedy and asked, "What do you think of that?" Kennedy replied, "It sounds like another one of Rusk's corn stories."

During his meeting with Premier Khrushchev in Vienna, President Kennedy noticed a medal on Khrushchev's chest and asked what it was. The Premier replied that the medal was the Lenin Peace Prize. "I hope you keep it," Mr. Kennedy commented.

At their Vienna meeting on June 3, 1961, Premier Khrushchev told President Kennedy: "You're an old country, we're a young country."

"If you'll look across the table," the forty-four-year-old President quipped, "you'll see that we're not so old."

President Kennedy had heard that Canada's Prime Minister Lester B. Pearson was an expert in baseball statistics. Kennedy's good friend and assistant Dave Powers was also an avid baseball fan, so when Pearson came to Hyannis Port in 1963 the President saw an opportunity to have some fun.

The Prime Minister had come to discuss obtaining nuclear warheads for Canada, but when the men retired after dinner for the discussion, Pearson was startled to hear Kennedy bid Powers, "Dave, test him out."

Powers proceeded to question the Prime Minister rigorously on some of the more obscure bits of baseball lore and statistics, including batting averages, earned run percentages, and players' names. But Pearson came through beautifully, proving conclusively that his reputation was well founded. Kennedy took the whole scene in without a word, and finally satisfied, leaned back in his rocking chair and said, "He'll do." Rapport immediately established, the two heads of state then got down to business.

President Kennedy played host to President Ayub Khan of Pakistan at Mount Vernon. Secretary of the Interior Udall was chatting with President Ayub's daughter and told her that he once climbed a certain mountain in Pakistan. Unfortunately, Secretary Udall was mistaken; the mountain that he was referring to happened to be in neighboring Afghanistan. President Kennedy happened to overhear the Secretary's mistake and saved the situation by saying:

Madam, that is why I named Mr. Udall Secretary of the *Interior.*

On June 9, 1961, the following note was sent by President Kennedy to Prime Minister Diefenbaker of Canada after Mr. Diefenbaker has expressed his regrets over the fact that President Kennedy had sprained his back in a tree-planting ceremony on the President's recent visit to Canada.

Many thanks for your gracious message. The tree will be there long after the discomfort is gone.

The visit of India's Prime Minister Jawaharlal Nehru to the United States in 1961 was less than a success—due primarily to his taciturn and withdrawn mood. The situation was not helped by his first meeting with American reporters. Nehru was subjected to especially harsh and penetrating questions on television's "Meet the Press"—whose moderator was Lawrence Spivak. The following day the Prime Minister went to Washington for a state dinner with President Kennedy. On that occasion the President offered his ironic toast: "We all want to take this opportunity to welcome you to America, Mr. Prime Minister, though I doubt whether any words of mine can embellish the welcome already extended to you by Larry Spivak."

During Jawaharlal Nehru's visit to the United States, President Kennedy was somewhat taken aback by the Indian Prime Minister's frequent periods of silence. But when it was later mentioned to Kennedy that Nehru seemed to be interested and vivacious only when conversing with the First Lady, the President remarked, "A lot of our visiting statesmen have the same trouble."

The President once took visiting Prime Minister Nehru on a boat ride aboard the Honey Fitz *past the luxurious mansions of Newport, Rhode Island.*

As they passed the fashionable resort, the President turned to the Prime Minister and said:

I wanted you to see how the average American family lives.

On March 13, 1962, President Kennedy toasted the visiting President Ahidjo of the Cameroon, commenting:

He has done an extraordinary job—and so have the members of his government. He represents a country which is divided between those who speak English and French. He tells me that he addresses his Minister of Justice, who sits here, through an interpreter. I have the same problem very often. . . .

Following the state dinner that President and Mrs. Kennedy gave for the Shah of Iran and the Empress Farah, the President's toast began with "Ladies and Gentlemen: I know that you all join with me in welcoming our distinguished guests to the United States. His Highness and I have a 'burden' that we carry in common—we both paid state visits to Paris last year and from all accounts we might both as well have stayed at home."

June 3, 1961, marked the official meeting of the new American President and Premier Khrushchev in Vienna.

While discussing the ticklish question of a nuclear test ban, the President quoted an old Chinese proverb to Premier Khrushchev:

"The journey of a thousand miles begins with one step."

"You seem to know the Chinese very well," Premier Khrushchev commented.

"We may both get to know them better," answered Mr. Kennedy.

When he visited Germany, President Kennedy was met by enthusiastic crowds, causing him to comment in Bonn on June 23, 1963:

Chancellor Adenauer was generous enough to say that the outpouring was spontaneous, and I do believe there was spontaneous good will, but I cannot believe all of those flags they held in their hands came from their rooms and from their houses. As an old politician, somebody must have been working, Mr. Chancellor.

On June 3, 1963 President Radhakrishnan of India paid President Kennedy a visit at the White House. During dinner President Kennedy proposed a toast to Radhakrishnan, a distinguished former teacher and professor:

Here in the United States we have never gone so far, nor may I say to Professor Galbraith do we plan to go so far, as to make a professor the President of the United States. But we admire those countries that do.

In his toast to the visiting Prime Minister Gerhardsen of Norway, President Kennedy ironically observed:

It is almost sad that there are so few issues which are causing intense controversy between Norway and the United States—an unaccustomed feeling as I welcomed the Prime Minister here. We searched all morning in an attempt to find something that would cause "alarm" in both capitals. But, Prime Minister, we are very proud to have you here.

The White House
May 9, 1962

When President Houphouet-Boigny of the Ivory Coast visited the White House in 1962, President Kennedy offered this toast:

... I do not think that any visitor to our country has had a more constructive career than our distinguished guest of honor, and I am not alone referring to the fact that in a free election he was elected by 98 per cent of the voters of his country—a record which has not been equalled recently in the United States—and from all I read, will not be.

May 22, 1962

President Kennedy began his toast to the visiting Crown Prince Hassan of Libya with these words:

I want to express our very warm welcome to our distinguished guest who has been kind enough to come from his country to ours on his first visit to the United States. He proceeds from here to San Francisco, and then to New York. No distinguished visitor to this country ever asks to go to Boston or Austin. The Vice President and I are getting reconciled to that, with some difficulty.

October 16, 1962

When Chile's President Jorge Alessandri Rodriguez visited the White House on December 11, 1962, President Kennedy welcomed him with this ironic remark:

You come from a family which has been celebrated in the history of your country. The President told me this morning that he and two of his brothers were members of the Chilean Senate at the same time. My view is there shouldn't be such concentration, but he has survived it and maybe others will.

In January, 1961, shortly after his Inauguration, President Kennedy greeted Madame Hervé Alphand, wife of the French Ambassador, at a White House dinner:

Comment allez-vous? . . . My wife speaks good French, I understand only one out of five words, but always "De Gaulle."

V

Kennedy Abroad

ONE of John F. Kennedy's achievements as President was his ability to act as an ambassador of American good will while traveling abroad. Two factors contributed greatly to the success of his foreign travels: his lovely and charming wife, Jacqueline, and his own unfailing wit.

In Latin America and in Europe he endeared himself to millions with his off-the-cuff remarks and informal manner, despite the seriousness of his missions. But in Ireland, land of his ancestors, he really found a welcome. Judging by Kennedy's festive spirit throughout the trip, his return to Ireland may well have been one of the most pleasurable moments in his entire administration. It was surely a great and glad time for the Irish.

In this section you will find some of the quips and jokes that enlivened President Kennedy's visits around the globe.

On his first trip to Paris, in June, 1961, the President addressed the employees of the U.S. Embassy and remarked:

I tried to be assigned to the embassy in Paris myself, and unable to do so, I decided to run for President.

I do not think it entirely inappropriate to introduce myself to this audience. I am the man who accompanied Jacqueline Kennedy to Paris, and I have enjoyed it.

> *SHAPE Headquarters*
> *Paris, France*
> *June 2, 1961*

During his 1961 visit to France, President Kennedy's Quai d'Orsay suite had a gold bathtub. Upon noticing this extravagance, the President commented, "It may seem funny to us, but maybe it's a better use for gold than locking it up in Fort Knox."

This city is no stranger to me. A Parisian designed the city of Washington. He laid out our broad boulevards after living here in this community. When he had finished his generous designs, he presented a bill to the Congress for ninety thousand dollars, and the Congress of the United States, in one of those bursts of economic fervor, for which they are justifiably famous, awarded him the munificent sum of three thousand dollars. Some people have been so unkind as to suggest that your clothes designers have been collecting his bill ever since.

> *Paris, France*
> *June, 1961*

A few years ago it was said that the optimists learned Russian and the pessimists learned Chinese. I prefer to think that those with vision studied French and English.

Paris, France
June 1, 1961

President Kennedy's visit to Ireland was one of the high points in his life. His high good humor was evident throughout the trip. In Cork, after introducing his close friends Larry O'Brien and David Powers, he continued: "And now I would like to introduce to you the pastor at the church which I go to, who comes from Cork—Monsignor O'Mohoney. He is the pastor of a poor, humble flock in Palm Beach, Florida."

On June 29, 1963, President Kennedy greeted enthusiastic crowds in Galway, Ireland, with this quip:

How many of you have relatives in America whom you don't admit to? If you ever come to America, come to Washington and tell them, if they wonder who you are at the gate, that you come from Galway. The word will be out—it will be *Céad míle fáilte,* which means in Gaelic "a hundred thousand welcomes."

I am deeply honored to be your guest in the free Parliament of free Ireland. If this nation had achieved its present political and economic stature a century or so ago, my great grandfather might never have left New Ross and I might, if fortunate, be sitting down there with you. Of course, if your own President had never left Brooklyn, he might be standing up here instead of me. This elegant building as you know, was once the property of the Fitzgerald family but I have not come here to claim it. Of all the new relations I have discovered on this trip, I regret to say that no one has yet found any link between me and a great Irish patriot, Lord Edward Fitzgerald. Lord Edward, however, did not like to stay here in his family home because, as he wrote his mother, "Leinster House does not inspire the brightest ideas." That was a long time ago, however.

It has been said by some that a few of the features of this stately mansion served to inspire similar features in the White House in Washington. Whether this is true or nót, I know that the White House was designed by Hobin, a noted Irish-American architect, and I have no doubt that he believed by incorporating several features of the Dublin style he would make it more homelike for any President of Irish descent. It was a long wait, but I appreciate his efforts.

There's also an unconfirmed rumor that Hobin was never fully paid for his work on the White House. If this proves to be true, I will speak to our Secretary of the Treasury about it—although I hear this body is not particularly interested in the subject of revenues.

Irish Parliament
June, 1963

On his trip to Ireland, President Kennedy received honorary degrees from the two leading Irish universities, Trinity College and National University. Trinity is English and Protestant in tone and National University is historically Catholic. On June 28, 1963, after receiving his honorary degrees from the two universities, Mr. Kennedy quipped:

I want to say how pleased I am to have this association with these two great universities. I now feel equally part of both, and if they ever have a game of Gaelic football or hurling, I shall cheer for Trinity and pray for National.

I can imagine nothing more pleasurable than continuing day after day to drive through the streets of Dublin and wave—and I may come back and do it.

Dublin, Ireland
June 29, 1963

At a gathering in Wexford, Ireland, on June 29, 1963, Mr. Kennedy was presented with an engraved gold box. Expressing his gratitude, the President remarked:

I am proud to have connected, on that beautiful gold box, the coat of arms of Wexford, the coat of arms of the kingly and beautiful Kennedys, and the coat of arms of the United States. That is a very good combination.

About fifty years ago, an Irishman from New Ross traveled down to Washington with his family, and in order to tell his neighbors how well he was doing, he had his picture taken in front of the White House and said, "This is our summer home. Come and see it."

New Ross, Ireland
June 28, 1963

On his trip to Ireland, President Kennedy visited Duganstown on June 28, 1963, to see a third cousin, Mary Ryan, who prepared an elaborate buffet in his honor.

I want to thank all of those who prepared this. It was a great effort on their part. We can promise we will come only once every ten years.

I don't want to give the impression that every member of this administration in Washington is Irish. It just seems that way.

City Hall
Cork, Ireland
June 28, 1963

Mr. Mayor, I would like to have you meet the head of the American Labor movement, whose mother and father were born in Ireland—George Meany, who is traveling with us.

And I would like to have you meet the only man with us

who doesn't have a drop of Irish blood, but who is dying to:
the head of protocol of the United States, Angier Biddle
Duke.

Wexford, Ireland
June 28, 1963

When my great grandfather left here to become a cooper
in East Boston, he carried nothing with him except two
things, a strong religious faith and a strong desire for liberty.
And I'm glad to say that all of his great grandchildren have
valued that inheritance. If he hadn't left, I'd be working over
at the Albatross Company.

Ireland
June, 1963

*In remarks in Bonn, Germany, on June 23, 1963, President
Kennedy referred to the fact that German Chancellor Adenauer, one of the world's oldest statesmen, was still very
active despite his age:*

Carl Schurz wrote in his nineteenth-century memoirs that
his first public speech was an extemporaneous, public outburst to a crowd of his fellow students in the great university
hall of Bonn.

He related how one of his professors inquired his age and,
when told he was nineteen, remarked, "Too bad; still too
young for our new German Parliament." They have been
saying the same thing about your Chancellor for many
years.

Once again Berlin and the Federal Republic have spoiled us for home. Now, when we don't get a million people out for a political speech in Worcester, Massachusetts, or Danbury, Connecticut, everyone, especially the reporters, is going to write that there are signs of apathy in the United States. And when we have crowded dinners of fifty at the White House, I am afraid this dinner is going to throw a pall on the entire affair.

City Hall Luncheon
Berlin, Germany
June 26, 1963

On a state visit to France, President Kennedy attended the Paris ballet on the night of June 1, 1961, as the guest of President Charles De Gaulle. During the intermission, the Kennedys and their host retired to a theater anteroom. French photographers were let in, for a quick historical portrait, then dismissed with an imperious flick of a De Gaulle finger. "Don't you wish you could control your photographers like that?" a reporter asked Mr. Kennedy. President Kennedy remarked dryly:

You must remember that I wasn't recalled to office as *my* country's savior.

While on a state visit to Canada in June, 1961, the President met the wife of Canada's Defense Production Minister,

Raymond O'Hurley, who told the President that all her relatives in Ohio and Connecticut had voted for him.

The President smiled and remarked:

Well, with a name like O'Hurley, they should.

I feel at home here because I number in my own state of Massachusetts many friends and former constituents who are of Canadian descent. Their vote is enough to determine the outcome of an election, even a Presidential election. You can understand that having been elected President of the United States by less than 140 thousand votes out of 60 million, that I am very conscious of these statistics.

During his stay in Paris, President Kennedy made this reference to his ancestors: "I am the descendant on both sides of two grandparents who served in the city council of Boston, and I am sure they regarded that as a more significant service than any of their descendants have yet rendered."

VI

IV

The Kennedy Clan

THE members of John F. Kennedy's family, headed by the indomitable patriarch Joseph P. Kennedy, are an extremely close-knit group, in the old tradition. An ambitious and vigorous clan, they are always quick to help each other out, as shown by the spirited participation of every Kennedy in every campaign featuring a Kennedy as candidate.

It is said that John Kennedy would never have aspired to the Presidency, perhaps not to any public office at all, had his brother Joe, Jr., not been killed in World War II. Everyone who knew Joe had been confident that he would someday be President, almost as a matter of course. But when Joe was killed, John picked up the fallen baton, just as Robert F. Kennedy has done since John's death.

But even such close unity and loyalty did not exempt family members from the needling wit of John F. Kennedy. In fact, the clan's togetherness only made them more likely targets for the President's good-natured teasing. When John Kennedy had finally made up his mind to appoint his brother Robert Attorney General, and the two men were about to meet the press to make the formal announcement, John turned to Robert and muttered, "Damn it, Bobby, comb your hair and don't smile too much. They'll think we are happy about the appointment."

The warmth and humor of John Kennedy are nowhere better exemplified than in the wonderful witticisms in this next section.

President Kennedy's young daughter Caroline was the delight of the press. White House reporters continually commented on her daily activities, and she returned their affection with a candid talkativeness. When a Congressmen told Kennedy that his daughter had informed him that she didn't want to live in the White House, Kennedy replied: "That's not my problem with Caroline. My problem is to keep her from holding press conferences."

Ever since his brother began to serve as his campaign manager, the President had been receiving advice from seasoned politicians who considered Robert Kennedy too young for such a big job. The President had this to say to a group of worried Democratic leaders prior to the 1960 campaign:

If I need somebody older, there's no need to go outside of the family. I can always get my father.

Robert Kennedy dedicated his book, *The Enemy Within*, to his wife Ethel, explaining that her "love through this long period made the difficult easy, the impossible possible."

At Christmas, 1960, after John F. Kennedy had been elected President with the invaluable aid of his brother, John and Jacqueline gave Robert an especially bound red leather volume of *The Enemy Within*. The first page of the book bore this inscription from Mrs. Kennedy: "To Bobby—who made the impossible possible and changed all our lives. With love, Jackie."

But the sentiment and rhetoric of these inscriptions were too flowery for the ironic taste of John Kennedy. Below his wife's inscription the President-elect had written in his barely legible scrawl: "For Bobby—The Brother Within—who made the easy difficult. Jack, Christmas, 1960."

There was much discussion after the President appointed his brother Attorney General. Mr. Kennedy recognized the fact that in the beginning many people were against his decision. Shortly after his announcement, he joked:

Speaking of jobs for relatives, Master Robert Kennedy, who is four, came to see me today, but I told him we already had an Attorney General.

I want you to meet my sister, Pat Lawford, from California. Somebody asked her last week if I was her kid brother, so she knew it was time this campaign came to an end.

Manchester, New Hampshire
November 7, 1960

Once John Kennedy was playing the Hyannis Port golf course with his wife, Jackie. On the seventeenth hole he watched her vainly try to blast her ball out of a sand trap, on each try the exasperating ball trickling back to her feet. "Open the face of the club," he called from his golf cart. "Follow through." But it was of no avail. Finally he lost patience and, taking the club from Jackie announced, "Let me show you." After a couple of fluid practice swings, he brought the club back gracefully, then swung it down powerfully into and through the sand. The ball rose a good two feet and dribbled mockingly back into the sand. Without losing his poise for a moment, Kennedy handed the club back to Jackie and said, "See, that's how you do it."

This district was the first district to endorse me as a candidate for President, nearly a year ago. My family had not even endorsed me when you endorsed me.

Brooklyn, New York
October 27, 1960

I see nothing wrong with giving Robert some legal experience as Attorney General before he goes out to practice law.

Alfalfa Club
Washington, D.C.
January 21, 1961

On this matter of experience, I had announced earlier this year that if successful I would not consider campaign contributions as a substitute for experience in appointing Ambassadors. Ever since I made that statement I have not received one single cent from my father.

Alfred E. Smith Memorial Dinner
New York City
October 19, 1960

I want you to meet my sister, Pat Lawford. She is here for my wife who is home. We are having a baby in November— a boy.

Richmond, Virginia
September 8, 1960

QUESTION. As a Kentuckian, I married a Massachusetts girl. Can you state as evasively as Nixon would under the circumstances, which state, Kentucky or Massachusetts, produces the most beautiful women?

MR. KENNEDY. Taking a leaf out of the Vice-President's book, my wife comes from New York, and, therefore I would say that New York produces the most beautiful women.

Louisville, Kentucky
October 5, 1960

When shown a picture of his newest nephew in August, 1963, the President remarked:

He looks like a fine baby—we'll know more later.

When President Kennedy's brother Edward defeated House Speaker John McCormack's nephew Eddie in the Massachusetts senatorial race, the President was placed in a somewhat awkward position. The inevitable charges of nepotism did not ruffle him too much, but he was concerned that the outcome might strain his relations with the august Speaker. The President scrupulously avoided personal involvement in the election, but he quipped off the record to the Gridiron Club: "I have announced that no Presidential aide or appointee would be permitted to take part in that political war in Massachusetts. Of course, we may send up a few training missions. . . . All I can say is: I'd rather be Ted than Ed."

President Kennedy made these remarks at a dinner of the Gridiron Club. Referring to his sister-in-law, Princess Radziwell, President Kennedy said:

It is not true that we're going to change the name of Lafayette Square to Radziwell Square—at least, not during my first term.

In 1944, Mr. Kennedy sent the following note to his younger brother, Bobby, from the Solomon Islands:

The folks sent me a clipping of you taking the oath. The sight of you up there was really moving, particularly as a close examination showed that you have my checked London coat on.

I'd like to know what the hell I'm doing out here while you go stalking around in my drape coat, but I suppose that's what we are out here for, so that our sisters and younger brothers will be safe and secure. Frankly, I don't see it that way—at least if you're going to be safe and secure, that's fine with me, but not in my coat, brother.

When President Kennedy was deciding whether or not to appoint his brother Robert as Attorney General, most of his associates—including Bobby—advised against it. However, the President-elect made up his own mind, and when the decision had been made, he was asked by a confidant how he planned to announce the controversial appointment. Kennedy answered: "Well, I think I'll just open the front door of the Georgetown house some morning about 2:00 A.M., look up and down the street, and if there's no one there, I'll whisper 'It's Bobby.' " When the actual moment did arrive, and he and Robert started out the door to meet the press, John turned to his brother and said, "Damn it, Bobby, comb your hair and don't smile too much. They'll think we are happy about the appointment."

QUESTION. Due to the fact that your wife is going to have a baby and you are certain that it is going to be a boy, there are a lot of expectant fathers who would like to know your secret of knowing that it is going to be a boy.

MR. KENNEDY. She told me. You would have to ask her.

Turlock, California
September 9, 1960

QUESTION. I come from Yonkers. I have an entirely different question to ask tonight, and I think an awful lot of people in this room are interested. Are you hoping it is a boy?

MR. KENNEDY. Well, as a matter of fact, I am flying home tonight to try and find an answer to that question. But actually, I have a daughter, and I know it sounds terrible and treasonous, but I really don't mind having another daughter again if that is the way it goes.

Syracuse, New York
September 29, 1960

The President made reference to his efforts to persuade Americans to drink milk.

I am certainly enjoying being with you newsmen this evening. None of you know how tough it is to have to drink milk three times a day.

Washington, D.C.
February, 1962

Attorney General Robert F. Kennedy got into hot water with the State of Texas when he remarked that the war with Mexico was not a very bright page in the history of the United States. Shortly after making that remark, the Attorney General was asked if he had anything further to say about the Mexican War. Mr. Kennedy replied that he'd spoken to the President about the matter and that the President said he wasn't "going to muzzle me," but from now on all speeches on Texas should be cleared with the Vice-President.

March 4, 1962

I have just received the following telegram from my generous Daddy. It says, "Dear Jack: Don't buy a single vote more than is necessary. I'll be damned if I'm going to pay for a landslide."

Gridiron Dinner
Washington, D.C.
1958

I would like to introduce my sister, Eunice Shriver, who lives in Chicago. I have sisters living in all the key electoral states in preparation for this campaign.

Libertyville, Illinois
October 25, 1960

Shortly before an important conference with Secretary of Defense Robert McNamara during the Cuban missile crisis, the President noticed his daughter Caroline running across the White House lawn.

"Caroline," the President shouted, "have you been eating candy?"

There was no answer from the President's young daughter.

"Caroline," the President repeated, "have you been eating candy? Answer yes, no, or maybe."

In the last campaign most of the members of this luncheon group today supported my opponent—except for a very few who were under the impression that I was my father's son.

National Association of Manufacturers
December 6, 1961

I have been presented with this donkey by two young ladies down there for my daughter. My daughter has the greatest collection of donkeys. She doesn't even know what an elephant looks like. We are going to protect her from that knowledge.

John Kennedy most enjoyed spending time with his children. Father and children continually teased one another, and their closeness and affection was known by all. The President loved to tell children's stories—and Caroline was his most attentive listener. One day, while the two were sitting on the stern of their boat, the *Honey Fitz*, Kennedy began to tell her a story about a huge white whale that lived in the ocean. Sitting next to President Kennedy was Franklin Roosevelt, Jr. His shoes were off, and he had on an old and dirty pair of sweatsocks. The President continued with the whale story, telling Caroline that one of the greatest delicacies for this whale was old, dirty sweatsocks. With this he reached over and snatched a sock off Roosevelt's foot and threw it overboard. Without pausing or cracking his deadpan, the President continued by relating that the only thing the strange creature liked *better* was a second sock, whereupon he again reached over, grabbed the second sock, and threw *it* blandly over the stern.

I come here to Florida today where my family has lived for thirty years, where they have already voted for one of the two candidates, and I feel it looks pretty good to get at least two votes in Florida.

Miami, Florida
October 18, 1960

President Kennedy made a practice of never discussing his official day when he was in his private quarters in the White House with his family.

However, once, a few years after he became President, Mrs. Kennedy asked her husband what kind of day it was.

The President shook his head and mentioned ten things which had gone wrong throughout the morning, "And," he added, "the day is only half over."

On a tour of Fort Bragg to inspect the new United States Special Forces, which had been especially organized for guerilla warfare, Mr. Kennedy noted the green berets that the Special Forces men were wearing and remarked:

I like those berets. The Special Forces need something to make them distinctive. My father even wears one now.

Ladies and gentlemen, Paul Douglas, the present U.S. Senator, and the next U.S. Senator, Hayes Beall, candidate for the Congress from this district, and my sister, Eunice, Mrs. Sargent Shriver, who lives in Illinois. One of my sisters is married to someone who lives in New York, one in California. We realized long ago we have to carry New York, Illinois, and California.

Elgin, Illinois
October 25, 1960

I want to express my great appreciation at the opportunity to be here with you, and to express my thanks to all of you for having attended this [Youth Fitness] Conference. I asked those members of the Cabinet who felt they were physically fit to come here today and I am delighted that Mr. Udall and Mr. Robert Kennedy and Governor Ribicoff responded to the challenge.

In June, 1961, a few days after a national magazine had referred to Bobby Kennedy as "the man with the greatest influence at the White House," the President received a call in his office from the Attorney General. Turning to a guest as he put his hand over the phone mouthpiece, Mr. Kennedy quipped:

This is the second most powerful man in the nation calling.

In July, 1961, after he noticed a story in a national magazine which said that the Kennedy brothers were "clothes-conscious," the President telephoned a reporter for the magazine and said:

What do you mean, the clothes-conscious Kennedy brothers? I may be but I don't think Bobby is. I don't think Bobby is very well-dressed, do you? Why, he still wears those button-down shirts. They went out five years ago. The only people I know who still wear them are Chester [Bowles] and Adlai.

In July, 1953, at the age of 36, John Kennedy had decided to change his marital status, and wrote the following to his close friend Paul Fay, Jr.:

I gave everything a good deal of thought—so am getting married this fall. This means the end of a promising political career as it has been based up to now almost completely on the old sex appeal.

QUESTION: Mr. President, the people of Florida are hoping that you and your family will again spend Christmas with them. Can you tell us what your present plans are, sir?

PRESIDENT KENNEDY: My mother and father are going to Florida in December and my wife and children hope to be there for Christmas and if my situation permits, I will go at Christmas. If the question is the result of some stories that the tourist business in Florida is off because of our difficulties, I do not think it will be.

November 20, 1962

I will introduce myself. I am Teddy Kennedy's brother, and I'm glad to be here tonight.

Democratic Rally
Harrisburg, Pennsylvania
September 20, 1962

QUESTION: Mr. President, it has been a long time since a President and his family have been subjected to such a heavy barrage of teasing and fun-poking and satire. There have been books on Backstairs at the White House and cartoon books with clever sayings and photo albums with balloons and now there is a smash hit record. Can you tell us whether you read them and listened to them and whether they produced annoyment or enjoyment?

PRESIDENT KENNEDY: Annoyment. Yes, I have read them and listened to Mr. Meader's record, but I thought it sounded more like Teddy than it did me, so he's annoyed.

I would like to recall a speech which Franklin Roosevelt made in regard to his dog. He said, "These Republican leaders have not been content with attacks on me, or my wife or my brothers. No, not content with that, they now include my little girl's pony, Macaroni. Well, I don't resent such attacks but Macaroni does."

I got a telegram tonight which said, "in honor of your birthday, I believe that you should get a rise in pay." Signed "Roger" [Roger Blough, President of United States Steel]. "P.S. *My* birthday is next month."

At four o'clock tomorrow, we're going to have a rally here on Medical Care for the Aged. Those who would prefer to stay and wait will find us all back here at the same stand.

And in the meanwhile, let me tell you what a pleasure it is once in a while to get out of Washington and not read the papers but come and see the voters.

New York's Birthday Salute to President Kennedy
Madison Square Garden
May 19, 1962

I want you to meet my sister, Patricia Lawford, who had the somewhat limited judgment to move from Massachusetts and come to Los Angeles.

Los Angeles, California
September 9, 1960

John F. Kennedy describing his first meeting at a dinner with Jacqueline Bouvier (Mrs. Kennedy):

I leaned across the asparagus and asked her for a date.

During the hard-fought and crucial West Virginia primary, President Kennedy's youngest brother, Ted, had just finished giving an enthusiastic speech in which he had said, "Do you want a man who will give the country leadership? Do you want a man who has vigor and vision?" When candidate Jack Kennedy took the microphone from his young brother, he opened his remarks by saying:

I would like to tell my brother that you cannot be elected President until you are thirty-five years of age.

I appreciate your being here this morning.

Mrs. Kennedy is organizing herself. It takes her longer, but, of course, she looks better than we do when she does it.

Fort Worth, Texas
November, 1963

Addressing a gathering of friends and relatives in Wexford, Ireland, Mr. Kennedy remarked:

It is my pleasure to be back from whence I came. Many people are under the impression that all the Kennedys are in Washington, but I am happy to see so many present who have missed the boat.

June 28, 1963

VII

IV

John F. Kennedy Meets the Press

JOHN F. KENNEDY's press conferences were a delight. The President usually showed up extremely well on these broadcast events, having made certain that he was well-versed on all the facts and figures relating to questions he was likely to encounter.

Moreover, the stimulation of the dialogue with the press often produced some of Kennedy's most memorable quips. Unexpected personal questions, or predictable queries asked in unexpected ways, often provoked unpredictable but comic responses from the fast-thinking President. Even guardedly hostile or trick questions, which aroused his spirit and his love of a good verbal fight, stirred Kennedy's wit.

This final chapter records some of the most hilarious moments of President Kennedy's press conferences.

On May 9, 1962, President Kennedy was asked to comment on the press treatment of his administration thus far:

Well, I'm reading more and enjoying it less.

QUESTION: Two books have been written about you recently. One of them has been criticized as being too uncritical of you and the other, by Victor Lasky, as being too critical of you. How would you review them—if you've read them?

PRESIDENT KENNEDY: I haven't read all of Mr. Lasky. I've just gotten the flavor of it. I see it's been highly praised by Mr. Drummond, Mr. Krock, and others. I'm looking forward to reading it, because the part that I read was not as brilliant as I gather the rest of it is from what they say about it.

At a press conference in February of 1961, a reporter asked Mr. Kennedy what steps the Government was considering to stop Cuban exports to this country. He specifically mentioned the shipment of molasses. After discussing the general problem, the President turned to the subject of molasses. He paused for a moment and said:

I believe it's going to be made into gin—and I'm not sure that's in the public interest.

QUESTION: There's a feeling in some quarters, sir, that big business is using the stock market slump as a means of forcing you to come to terms with business. One reputable columnist, after talking to businessmen, obviously, reported this week their attitude is "now we have you where we want you." Have you seen any reflection of this attitude?

PRESIDENT KENNEDY: I can't believe I'm where big business wants me.

QUESTION: Mr. President, this being Valentine's Day, sir, do you think it might be a good idea if you would call Senator Strom Thurmond of South Carolina down to the White House for a heart-to-heart talk over what he calls your defeatist foreign policy?

PRESIDENT KENNEDY: Well, I think that that meeting should probably be prepared at a lower level.

In November, 1961, President Kennedy was asked to comment about the election of Mayor Robert F. Wagner of New York and Governor Hughes of New Jersey. The reporters wanted to know if the President felt that since both Mayor Wagner and Governor Hughes were Democrats that their election indicated that things looked good for the Democrats in future elections.

They won because they were effective candidates. But they ran as Democrats. And I believe that indicates that the American people believe that the candidates and parties in those areas, as well as nationally, are committed to progress. So I am happy, and I suppose some day we will lose and then I'll have to eat those words.

QUESTION: Mr. President, you have said, and I think more than once, that heads of government should not go to the summit to negotiate agreements but only to approve agreements negotiated at a lower level. Now it's being said and written that you're going to eat those words and go to a summit without any agreement at a lower level. Has your position changed, sir?

PRESIDENT KENNEDY: Well, I'm going to have a dinner for all the people who've written it and we'll see who eats what.

March 7, 1962

QUESTION: I wonder if you could tell us whether if you had to do it over again you would work for the Presidency and whether you would recommend the job to others?

PRESIDENT KENNEDY: Well, the answer to the first is yes and the answer to the second is no. I don't recommend it to others, at least not for a while.

QUESTION: Mr. President, you once told us you had an opinion as to whether Mr. Nixon should enter the race for the California governorship, but you never did tell us what that was.

PRESIDENT KENNEDY: I think I said at the time that I would be glad to confide it to him, and he just has not, as yet, spoken to me about it. I'll be glad to come back to California and talk to him about it.

On November 29, 1961, during a Presidential press conference that President Kennedy received the news that the United States had successfully launched a chimpanzee into space. The President interrupted the press conference to announce the event to the assembled reporters:

This chimpanzee who is flying in space took off at 10:08. He reports that everything is going perfectly and working well.

QUESTION: Mr. President, Congressman Alger of Texas criticized Mr. Salinger as a young and inexperienced White House publicity man, and questioned the advisability of having him visit the Soviet Union. I wonder if you have any comment?

PRESIDENT KENNEDY: I know there are always some people who feel that Americans are always young and inexperienced and foreigners are always able and tough and great negotiators. But I don't think that the United States would have acquired its present position of leadership in the free world if that view were correct. Now, he also, as I saw the press, said that Mr. Salinger's main job was to increase my standing in the Gallup polls. Having done that, he's now moving on to improve our communications.

QUESTION: What did you think, sir, of the rather harsh things that Republican Congressman Boyle of Virginia had to say about you and your Press Secretary because Mr. Salinger gave a party last night for his Democratic opponent?

PRESIDENT KENNEDY: Well, I can see why he would be quite critical of that. But I will say that I never read as much about a Congressman in the papers as I do about that Congressman and see less legislative results.

QUESTION: Mr. President, some time ago you said that you were reading more now but enjoying it less. Do you have any more current observations on American journalism or on your personal reading habits?

PRESIDENT KENNEDY: No, I want to say that I am looking forward to all of you coming to the White House this afternoon between six and seven. Mr. Arthur Krock wrote of the temptations and seductions which take place in the press in the White House. But I want you to know that we expect that you will all emerge with your journalistic integrity and virtue unmarred. You will be courteous to the host on all occasions but it is not necessary that your views be changed.

American Society of Newspaper Editors
Washington, D.C.
April 19, 1963

QUESTION: There have been published reports that some high-placed Republican people have been making overtures to your Secretary of Defense for him to be their 1968 candidate for President. If you thought that Mr. McNamara were seriously considering these overtures, would you continue him in your cabinet?

PRESIDENT KENNEDY: I have too high a regard for him to launch his candidacy yet.

January 25, 1963

QUESTION: Mr. President, last Friday, John Bailey, the Democratic National Chairman made a speech in which he accused Governor Rockefeller of racial prejudice toward Negroes. And I wonder if you felt, even in an election year, that this was a justified statement?

PRESIDENT KENNEDY: No, I've never seen any evidence that Mr. Rockefeller is prejudiced in any way toward any racial group, and I'm glad to make that statement, and I'm sure that some of the statements that the Chairman of the Republican Committee has made about me will be similarly repudiated by leading Republicans. I've been waiting for it for about a year and a half.

QUESTION: Mr. President, now that the United States is being transmitted instantaneously overseas via Telstar, do you think the U.S. networks should make a greater effort to do something about the "vast wasteland"?

PRESIDENT KENNEDY: I'm going to leave Mr. Minow to argue the wasteland issue, I think.

July 24, 1962

QUESTION: Mr. President, have you narrowed your search for a new Postmaster General? And are you seeking a man with a business background or a political background?

PRESIDENT KENNEDY: The search is narrowing, but we haven't—there are other fields that are still to be considered, including even a postal background.

QUESTION: The Republican National Committee recently adopted a resolution saying you were pretty much of a failure. How do you feel about that?

PRESIDENT KENNEDY: I assume it passed unanimously.

July 17, 1963

QUESTION: Mr. President, what is your evaluation of Khrushchev's present status and the nature of the political struggle that is apparently now going on in the Kremlin?

PRESIDENT KENNEDY: I would think it is possible that Khrushchev is subjected to the same . . . I don't think we know precisely . . . but I would suppose he has his good months and bad months like we all do.

QUESTION: Mr. President, Senator Margaret Chase Smith has proposed that a watchdog committee be created. What is your reaction?

PRESIDENT KENNEDY: To watch Congressmen and Senators? Well, that will be fine if they feel they should be watched.

March 21, 1963

QUESTION: Mr. President, you have said that you are in favor of the two-term limit to the office of the Presidency. How do you feel about former President Eisenhower's suggestion that the terms of congressmen also be limited?

PRESIDENT KENNEDY: It's the sort of proposal which I may advance in a post-Presidential period, but not right now.